WHISPERS *of* WISDOM

Crafting Character through Mentorship and Storytelling Artistry

By
MASTER ANTONY GRAF

WHISPERS OF WISDOM

Crafting Character Through Mentorship and Story Telling

© All Rights Reserved. Copyright 2024 by Master Antony Graf

ALL RIGHTS RESERVED.

No part of this book or its associated ancillary materials may be reproduced or transmitted in any form or by any means, electronic or mechanical, including photocopying, recording, or by any information storage or retrieval system without permission of publisher.

FIRST EDITION

Book design by Saqib_arshad
Editing by Darcy Graf

Printed In the United States of America

CONTENTS

DEDICATION — 1

FORWARD BY: JUAN MIGUEL MORENO — 3

PART 1

STORYTELLING — 7
- Storytelling "The Why" — 9
- Storytelling "The How" — 10
- Story-Infused Actions: Creating Impactful Connections — 14
- Why It's Crucial to Read — 17
- The Story of Two Wolves for a Deeper Application of Our Fundamental Mentoring Principles — 17
- The Story of Two Wolves — 19

THE WOLF WE FEED — 21
- Cultivating Awareness of the Impact of Our Words: Pre-framing and Reframing — 23
- Negative and Positive Labeling: Being Conscious of Our Words — 25
- Seek to Understand — 28
- Understanding The 'Six Human Needs' — 30
- Understanding the Concept of the Five Love Languages for Children — 32

EMPOWER AWARENESS — 35
- Six Forms of Manipulation and Testing — 37
- 'Who is Training Whom?' — 39
- Essential Guidelines for Effective Discipline — 41

FUNDAMENTAL COMMUNICATION STRATEGIES — 45
- It isn't What They Say About You it's What They Whisper — 47
- What Is Praise-Correct-Praise? — 50
- Coaching in the Wanted Behavior — 52

Catching your Child Being Good	55
Praising Children for Effort Over Ability	58
Leading with Empathy	61
Audio, Visual, Kinesthetic: The three Primary Ways People Absorb Information	65
Memorable Communication	67

EMOTIONAL GUIDANCE — 71

Addressing the Fight or Flight Response in Children	73
Transforming Anger	77
ANTs — Automatic Negative Thoughts	79
A Process for Transforming a Negative Belief	81

SELF-FULFILLING PROPHECIES — 85

We are the Type of People Who" The Impact Tribe and Beliefs	87
The Power of "I am"	91
Attitude of Gratitude	94
Power of Symbolism and Rituals	97

PREPARING FOR TRIUMPH — 99

Intrinsic Motivation vs. Extrinsic Motivation: What Drives Us to Act?	101
Nurturing Success through Habits, Routine, and Environment	104
"Creating Artificial Challenges for Strength and Resilience"	106

PART 2

ANGER, REACTION AND STUBBORNNESS — 111

The Fence: Anger	113
How to Hunt a Monkey: Stubbornness	115
The Cockroach Theory	117
Potato, Egg, Coffee bean: Reaction	119
The Pencil: Be the Best You Can Be	121

TRUST LIES BOASTING — 123

The Scorpion and the Frog : Trust and Nature	124
The Boy Who Cried Wolf: Never Lie	126
The Pheasant and the Bull: Self-Deception	128
The Four Students: Lies and Truth	130
Monkey and the Dolphin: Bragging	131

THE JOURNEY AND BEING PRESENT   133

    Special Olympians: More Than Winning   135
    Life is a Race Motivational Short Story: Enjoying the Journey   137
    Being and Breathing: Just being   139

THE POWER OF WORDS AND INTENTIONS   141

    The Rice Experiment: The Power of Intentions   142
    The Dog's Reflections: The power of Intentions   144
    Mark Twain: Think Before You Speak   146
    Toothpaste: Think Before You Speak   148

THINKING OF OTHERS AND TEAMWORK   151

    Rabbit and the Fish: Thinking of Others   153
    Find Happiness - Thinking of Others/Team Work   154
    Strength In Unity: Team Work   156

KINDNESS   158

    The Lion and The Mouse: Kindness   159
    Saving Sand Dollars: Kindness and Proactivity   161
    Scrubbing Turtles: Kindness and Proactivity   162
    Androcles and the Lion: Kindness   164
    Angry Dog: Compassion   165

POSITIVE OUTLOOK AND HAPPINESS   167

    $100: Self-Love   169
    The Cracked Pot: Self-Love   171
    The Two Shoe Salesman: Optimism   173
    Put Down the Negativity: Happiness   175
    Attitude is Everything: Optimism   177
    Two Tigers: Comparison   179
    A Dog Without a Job: Nature, Purpose and Happiness   180

POWER OF BELIEF   183

    The Elephant Rope: Limiting Beliefs   185
    Jumping Frogs: The Effect of Beliefs   187
    Swimming Experiment: Power of Belief   189
    Roger Bannister: Breaking Limiting Beliefs   190

LIFE HAPPENS FOR ME AND GROWTH — 193

Kintsugi: Tragedy — 194
"Helping" a Butterfly: Growth — 196
The Lobster: Growth — 198
Maybe: Life Happens for Me — 200
The Burning Hut: Life Happens for Me — 202

PROXIMITY — 205

Monkey Experiment: Blind Adherence. — 207
Raised By Chickens: Proximity — 209

PERSEVERANCE AND AN UNBREAKABLE SPIRIT — 211

Digging For Gold: Perseverance — 212
The Two Mice in the Bucket of Cream: Perseverance /Unbreakable Spirit — 214
The Donkey Who Fell Down a Well: Perseverance/Unbreakable Spirit — 216
The Unbreakable Runner: Perseverance/Unbreakable Spirit — 218

TAKING ACTION — 221

Socrates and the Secret to Success: Burning Desire — 223
Take the Leap Riddle: Take Action — 225
Rock in the Road: Take Action — 227
A Wise Man's Jokes: Take Action — 229
Nothing Comes from Nothing: Take Action/Proactivity — 231
The Power of Visualization: Take Action-Outside the Box — 233

CONSISTENCY EFFORT HARD WORK AND PREPARATION — 235

Carpenter's Retirement: Effort — 236
Two Lumberjacks: Preparation — 238
The Tortoise and the Hare: Hard Work and Consistency — 240
The Crow and the Pitcher: Hard Work and Consistency. — 242
Soar Like an Eagle: Lean into Hard Work — 243

PROCRASTINATION AND NEGLIGENCE — 245

Frogs for Dinner: Procrastination — 247
Mouse In the Rice: Procrastination — 249
A Snowball Effect: Negligence — 250

WHISPERS of WISDOM

DEDICATION

There is no such thing as a self-made man. I am most grateful for the emotional challenges I went through as a child. Like most children, I often felt inadequate. I am grateful for all those challenges as they have created the drive that has given me the purpose to provide tools to parents. My destiny has taken me through the fire and created a desire and resilience inside me that propelled me to the top in many areas of my life.

I'm grateful to my parents who instilled a tremendous work ethic and intensity, leading by example. If you're going to do something, you should do it right. My mentors, Peter Bardatsos, Juan Moreno, Han Won Lee, Herbert Perez, Kevin Padilla, and Mark Williams, each in their own way, impacted my life tremendously with words of encouragement, wisdom, and old-school trial by fire. I love them and truly feel that I carry pieces of them with me every day in my teachings.

Thank you, Tim Thackery and Jason Han, for bringing me to the next level and forcing me to organize my passion.

My 'Chosen Family' GM Paul Melella, Rachel & Nonito Donaire, Michael Bank, Cheong Park, your families continue to be the village that loves and uplifts me daily.

I am deeply grateful for my incredible students and top-notch instructors, Lyles Moore and Jose Miguel. The Believe Martial Arts community is the driving force behind my continuous pursuit of improvement each day.

My two children, Titan and Athena, each drive me to do amazing things. I am fueled by the idea that I must lead by example. You may not realize it, but knowing that I am one of the primary role models in your life is a job I take very seriously. You make me live my life to the highest standard of values, fitness, resilience, and work ethic, all because "I refuse to be a hypocrite." I cannot inspire and give advice on things that I am not doing myself, and for that, I thank you. I love you with all my heart.

Finally, the love of my life, the one who fills my cup every day to ensure that I am overflowing with love and joy to better the universe and live my purpose. I am beyond grateful for you, my wife, Darcy Graf.

FORWARD

By: Juan Miguel Moreno

3x Olympian, 2x Olympic Silver Medalist and one of the most decorated Olympic Coaches in the history of TAEKWONDO

Master Antony Graf, or "Tony," has been a standout figure in my life since our first encounter. In fact, I would say he is one of my favorite people in the entire world. I first met Tony during his teenage years as an emerging athlete. What struck me was his directness, but what made an impression on me was the emotion and passion he had in the "moment." Tony made direct eye contact, had immediate responses to my questions, and exuded joyfulness in the present moment that left a lasting impression.

Years later, Tony joined my Taekwondo team in Miami, arriving with modest means but with an abundance of personal expectations. Despite lacking in stature and inherent abilities, his unparalleled passion and emotion propelled him to greatness in our sport. Tony's unparalleled work ethic, intense focus, and willingness to embrace all challenges eventually defined his athletic career.

Beyond his athletic achievements, Tony seamlessly transitioned into teaching martial arts. This was considered a normal progression for him, but what most didn't know was if this lone wolf athlete could become a leader of a pack for society to follow. Amazingly, Tony has emerged as an authority on character development, evident in his book "Whispers of Wisdom." Tony's direct, simple approach offers a practical guide for cultivating character in today's society, making it a valuable resource for anyone invested in shaping the future of the people they truly care about. Tony's "Whispers of Wisdom" will undoubtedly become your step-by-step resource for practically any personality type that you encounter.

PREFACE

As a preface to understanding the practices outlined in this book, please note that part one introduces mentoring tools, skills, and drills aimed at fostering improved habits, behaviors and relationships with children. Part two consists of a collection of timeless tales categorized by morals, values, and lessons. This compilation serves as a handbook, allowing you to select stories at any time to meet the needs of specific situations or values you wish to instill in those you are mentoring.

STORYTELLING

- Storytelling "The Why"
- Storytelling "The How"
- Story-Infused Actions: Creating Impactful Connections
- Why It's Crucial to Read: The Story of Two Wolves for a Deeper Application of Our Fundamental Mentoring Principles.
- The Story of Two Wolves
  The Wolf We Feed

Storytelling "The Why"

Leaders use storytelling as a powerful tool to influence, coach, and inspire because stories connect people and ideas. They convey culture, history, and values, creating ties that bind us in countries, communities, and families. In coaching and parenting, stories solidify relationships and firmly anchor values and concepts altogether.

Good stories not only create a sense of connection but also build familiarity and trust. They make listeners more open to learning, offering multiple meanings in an engaging way. For instance, in a coaching session, a story about overcoming challenges is more impactful than just presenting a list of strategies.

Storytelling works for all learners - visual, auditory, and kinesthetic. Stories stick in memory, as research shows they're remembered more accurately and longer than facts alone. Stories are a serious coaching tool, influencing attitudes and behaviors effectively.

Stories about personal mistakes, overcoming challenges, or instilling overall positive values are great for learning and inspiring. People identify closely with stories, making learning risk-free. Coaches and parents sharing timeless and classic or personal stories convey values, offer insights, and inspire, making storytelling a powerful way for leaders to influence, inspire, and teach in coaching and parenting roles.

Storytelling "The How"

As an example of interactive storytelling, here is a step-by-step guide on how to tell the story of the donkey who fell down the well:

Start by telling all the children that it's crucial to keep their eyes on you during the story, emphasizing that it helps them become better listeners. Promise them that it will enhance their ability to remember the tale. Begin with, "There once was a donkey who fell down a well. There once was a donkey who fell down a..." leaving room for them to complete the word "well."

Describe the donkey as old and the well as old as well. Explain that the farmer, who owned it, deemed it too much work to rescue the donkey and decided to cover it up. Express concern with an enthusiastic "Oh no."

Continue the story as the farmer picks up a shovel. Pantomime shoveling and throwing dirt on the donkey's back, prompting the donkey to cry, "Hee haw, hee haw." Repeat this action, involving the children in the pantomime and sound effects. The farmer repeats this a third time, and now the donkey confidently says (he haw! - with confidence and intent).

Describe the donkey shaking off the dirt and ask the children to demonstrate how they would shake off dirt. Next, mention stomping it down, having the children act it out, and finally, stepping up, asking the children to demonstrate stepping up. Repeat this process twice more, involving the children in both actions and speech.

Conclude with the donkey jumping out of the well, asking the children to show how they would jump out. Emphasize that the donkey never gave up. Repeat the sentence and encourage the children to finish the sentence; for example, saying never give... And the children say, "up!"

Finish with the moral: In life, people will say mean things to you. If they do, shake it off and step. Have the children finish with the word "up." In life, things will be challenging. When they are, shake it off and step. Have the children finish with the word "up!"

You can finish the story by interacting with your child/children, asking them what their favorite part was or what they learned about this story.

Storytelling is a collaborative endeavor, and encouraging active participation is key. Let's break down steps to make this interactive experience impactful:

1. **Eye Contact Encouragement:**
    - When speaking to a child or a group, prioritize eye contact to establish a personal connection.
    - Begin by pre-framing the importance of attentive listening, emphasizing the significance of the storyteller relaying information.
    - Show appreciation for their attention, setting the stage for an engaged storytelling session.

2. **Interactive Engagement Techniques:**
    - Encourage participation by inviting children to finish sentences or repeat key elements of the story.
    - Create anticipation by leaving open spaces for their responses. For instance, after introducing a story element, pause and allow them to complete the sentence.

3. **Repetition Reinforcement:**
   - Reinforce the story's structure through repetition. Have children repeat key phrases, enhancing comprehension and memory.

4. **Managing Enthusiastic Interruptions:**
   - Acknowledge a child's excitement to engage with the story while maintaining the narrative flow.
   - If they try to speak out of turn, gently interrupt by snapping fingers and pointing (as if you were saying "just a moment".
   - Politely inform them it's not their turn yet and assure them they will have an opportunity to share.

5. **Multisensory Storytelling:**
   - Utilize vivid language and descriptive details to engage children's imagination.
   - Incorporate expressive voices for characters, employing different tones and pitches to make the story more captivating.

6. **Engaging Visual Aids:**
   - Enhance comprehension by using props, illustrations, or simple drawings to complement the story visually.

7. **Sound Effects for Immersion:**
   - Make storytelling a multisensory experience by adding simple sound effects or encouraging children to create them.

8. **Physical Participation:**
   - Foster physical engagement by letting children act out parts of the story. This promotes a deeper connection to the narrative.

9. **Relatability and Connection:**
   - Connect the story to children's own experiences, making it more relatable and facilitating better understanding.

10. Timing and Complexity Consideration:
» Be mindful of attention spans, keeping stories appropriately timed and adjusting complexity based on age.

11. Moral Emphasis and Takeaways:
» If relevant, include a clear moral or lesson in the story, reinforcing positive values and providing a meaningful takeaway for the child.

By incorporating these steps, storytelling becomes a dynamic and engaging group activity, fostering both enjoyment and retention for children.

Story-Infused Actions: Creating Impactful Connections
Attaching a story to an action to make a deeper connection.

When you attach a story to an action, it makes it more impactful. For example, as a child, when I shook hands, my father would always tell me to shake hand firmly. At first, I didn't think much about it and would give a sloppy fish handshake. It didn't connect until my uncle, who had military training, would crush my hand every time he saw me. Little did I know he was priming me to learn a great lesson. He eventually showed me a technique to neutralize the grip by touching two fingers to the center of the wrist. This shifted my perspective on handshakes and gave them purpose. Now, I share this story and teach my students the "tigers paw" handshake, explaining it's purpose in preventing hand crushing but also fostering a sense of tribe/community and purpose connected to our "secret handshake"

Additionally, my father advised me to look in someone's eyes, but it never stuck. Teaching children, I would tell them to pick one eye because we can't look in both simultaneously. However, it wasn't deep enough and it didn't stick, so I had to look further and I found some neurological research that revealed looking into the left eye create an emotional connection tied to childhood experiences. The story goes like this: when we are infants, most mothers carry their children in their left hand to free up their right hand for daily chores. So, when they looked down at you, they were looking into your left eye. When you look into someone's left eye, it triggers a deeper connection ingrained in us when we were infants. This story resonates by addressing our deep human need for love and connection, thus being way more impactful because we attached a why and a purpose.

Whatever you teach, attaching a purpose and a story makes it more powerful. In our electronic generation, where human interaction is diminishing, focusing on understanding gestures, mannerisms, and basic courtesy with a meaningful narrative becomes crucial. To make concepts stick, use statistics, personal stories, or fables to provide a lasting impact, emphasizing the why, purpose and memorability. This approach can be applied to safety, basic human interaction, behaviors, or even mental health.

Simple example of actions where stories can be applied to make a deeper connection.

- Mealtime habits
- Share a story about family dinners, emphasizing the joy and connection fostered during shared meals.
- Highlight cultural traditions or personal experiences that make mealtime a special and meaningful part of the day.
- Illustrate the significance of healthy eating habits through stories that portray the positive impact on overall well-being.

*See Story: Strength in unity

- Smiling when you meet somebody.
- Narrate anecdotes that showcase the power of a smile in creating a positive and welcoming atmosphere.
- Share personal experiences where a simple smile led to a meaningful connection or improved someone's day.

- Emphasize the cultural or universal importance of smiling as a non-verbal communication tool that transcends language barriers.

See Story Section On: Optimism/seeing the good/happiness

- Importance of consistency in physical activity.
- Tell stories that highlight the benefits of consistent physical activity, focusing on personal growth and well-being.
- Share narratives of individuals who achieved success or overcame challenges by maintaining a regular exercise routine.
- Emphasize the long-term positive effects of consistency in physical activity, both for physical health and mental well-being.

See Story Section On: Consistency / effort/ hardwork/ preparation.

Why It's Crucial to Read:
The Story of Two Wolves for a Deeper Application of Our Fundamental Mentoring Principles.

Before diving into our mentoring section, it is imperative that you read the story of two wolves. This story serves as the foundational template that fuels all of my teaching and parenting principles.

The general concept is simple: the behaviors, actions, and habits that we feed will grow.

Simply put, where your attention goes, your child grows.

Creating awareness of you and your child's actions by studying the guidelines will help consciously strengthen the values we wish to instill in our children.

In my own life, I constantly remind myself of the principles from the story of two wolves to make a conscious effort to pair them with these fundamental mentoring tools.

The Story of Two Wolves

An elder Native American was teaching a group of children about life. He said to them, "A fight is going on inside me. It is a terrible fight between two wolves. One wolf is a bad wolf, and represents fear, anger, envy, sorrow, regret, greed, arrogance, self-pity, guilt, resentment, inferiority, lies, false pride, superiority, and ego. The other is a good wolf, and stands for joy, peace, faith, hope, sharing, serenity, humility, kindness, friendship, empathy, generosity, truth, compassion, and love. This same fight is going on inside of you, and every other person."

The old man was silent, and let the students consider this for a few minutes. Eventually a child spoke, and asked the elder, "Which wolf will win the fight?"

The teacher simply replied, "The one that we feed the most."

The Moral

Within each person, there is a constant internal struggle between positive and negative qualities. The outcome of this internal battle depends on which qualities we choose to nourish and cultivate in our lives. In essence, the story teaches that the one we feed—whether the good wolf or the bad wolf—will ultimately prevail in influencing our thoughts, actions, and overall character.

THE WOLF WE FEED

UNDERSTANDING THE IMPACT OF WORDS AND COMMUNICATING WITH OTHERS IN THE WAYS THE RECEIVE INFORMATION THE BEST

> Cultivating awareness of the impact of our words: Pre-framing and reframing.
> Negative and positive labeling, being conscious of our words.
> Seek to Understand
> Understanding The 'Six Human Needs'
> Understanding the Concept of the Five Love Languages for Children

Cultivating awareness of the impact of our words: Pre-framing and reframing

Our language shapes who we are, reflecting in the words and phrases we frequently use. Below are 30 examples illustrating how to pre-frame and reframe the words we commonly employ, whether it's in coaching, self-talk, or observing how others describe themselves. Familiarize yourself with this list. When we catch ourselves or others using negative words, take a moment to pause. Instead, reframe the language positively. It becomes even more impactful when we not only rephrase but also delve deeper, supporting the shift with quotes and stories.

For instance, if a child says "can't," intervene by expressing that it's not a matter of inability but rather a skill not yet mastered. Encourage persistence, affirming that they will grasp it with continued effort. A relevant quote by Teddy Roosevelt emphasizes the power of belief: "If you believe you can't, you're right; if you believe you can, you're also right." To further illustrate, share a story, such as the one about the baby elephant tied to a post (see page 179), highlighting the impact of limiting beliefs. Personal anecdotes from your own life can also foster empathy and a connection to the present situation.

1. Can't → I haven't mastered it yet or I can, but it's a work in progress.
2. Problem → Challenge or Opportunity for improvement.
3. Mistake → Learning experience or Stepping stone to success.
4. Failure → Setback or First attempt in learning.
5. Weakness → Area for growth or Potential strength.

6. Impossible → Possible with effort or Challenging, but doable.
7. Hate → Dislike or Prefer something else.
8. Stress → Pressure or Excitement about a busy day.
9. Rejected → Not selected this time or Opportunity for a better match.
10. Problematic → Not ideal or Something to address and improve.
11. Nervous → Excited or Eager anticipation.
12. Lazy → Relaxing or Taking a break.
13. Difficult → Challenging or Requires effort.
14. Confused → Curious or Seeking clarity.
15. Hurt → Uncomfortable or In need of healing.
16. Hopeless → Seeking solutions or Temporary setback.
17. Old-fashioned → Classic or Timeless.
18. Unimportant → Minor or Less critical at the moment.
19. Worthless → Valuable in different ways or Unique.
20. Unprepared → Getting ready or In the process of preparation.
21. Disorganized → Flexible or Exploring different approaches.
22. Stubborn → Persistent or Committed to my decision.
23. Gossip → Sharing information or Casual conversation.
24. Arrogant → Confident or Sure of oneself.
25. Quitting → Taking a break or Reassessing goals.
26. Depressed → Reflective or In a contemplative state.
27. Overwhelmed → Challenged or Facing a demanding situation.
28. Boring → Routine or Consistent.
29. Unmotivated → Exploring inspiration or Seeking new sources of motivation.
30. Disinterested → Selective or Choosing where to focus my interest.

Negative and Positive Labeling: Being Conscious of Our Words

The Negative Labeling Theory, a concept rooted in sociology and developed by Howard Becker in the 1960s, posits that assigning negative labels to individuals can profoundly impact their behavior and self-perception. In environments like schools, societal labels such as "troublemaker" or "problem child" can shape how others perceive and interact with individuals, subsequently influencing their self-image and actions. This theory emphasizes the potential harm of negative stereotypes, highlighting a self-fulfilling prophecy where individuals conform to the expectations set by these labels.

This notion aligns seamlessly with the understanding that words matter, particularly in the context of parenting. The words used when discussing children and their behavior hold substantial influence over their self-image. Remarkably, these words also shape parental thoughts, perspectives, and attitudes. By consciously choosing positive language and reframing descriptions, parents can alter how children perceive themselves and, in turn, foster healthier attitudes and higher self-esteem.

Re-framing, a powerful tool in this context, involves changing one's attitude and reactions without altering the behavior or situation itself. By describing a child's behavior more positively and with greater understanding, parents can encourage a more constructive outlook. For instance, instead of labeling a child as "unpredictable," they can re-frame this as being "flexible" or a "creative problem solver."

The synergy between the Negative Labeling Theory and the acknowledgment that words matter underscores the significance of positive language. It offers a means to break the cycle of negative expectations, promoting an environment that nurtures healthier attitudes and fosters positive self-esteem in children. Ultimately, the way we communicate with and about children plays a pivotal role in shaping their self-perception and behavior.

Here's a list of 28 choices to replace common disempowering words with empowering words

1. Strong-Willed → Determined, Resilient
2. Stubborn → Persistent, Tenacious
3. Wild → Energetic, Adventurous
4. Emotional/Dramatic → Expressive, Passionate
5. Unpredictable → Spontaneous, Creative
6. Talkative → Communicative, Sociable
7. Quiet → Thoughtful, Reflective
8. Forceful → Assertive, Confident
9. Clingy → Affectionate, Attached
10. Bossy → Leadership Skills, Organized
11. Intense → Focused, Driven
12. Loud → Enthusiastic, Expressive
13. Impatient → Eager, Enthusiastic
14. Dreamy → Imaginative, Creative
15. Hyper-Sensitive → Perceptive, Empathetic
16. Shy → Thoughtful, Observant
17. Aggressive → Assertive, Ambitious
18. Fussy → Meticulous, Detail-Oriented

19. Serious → Thoughtful, Responsible
20. Troublesome/Restless → Energetic, Active
21. Brooding → Reflective, Thoughtful
22. Spirited → Energetic, Vibrant
23. Persistent → Determined, Tenacious
24. Energetic → Dynamic, Active
25. Bad Kid → Child with Challenging Behaviors
26. Unfocused → Exploring Diverse Interests
27. Always Misbehaves → Displays Independent Spirit
28. Annoying → Expressive and Energetic

Using positive language reframes the perception of these characteristics and fosters a more encouraging and supportive environment for a child's development.

Seek to Understand

As a mentor, it's important to understand what drives people. Tony Robbins' six human needs and the five love languages help us grasp these fundamental aspects.

Tony Robbins' six human needs teach us that everyone has core requirements that drive them toward fulfillment and it's crucial to meet these needs individually. This understanding shapes our approach to connect effectively with others.

The five love languages add another layer to communication. Recognizing how others receive love and appreciation allows us to adjust our style, creating a deeper connection based on their preferences.

When mentoring, it is my ultimate goal to communicate in a way that resonates with individuals. To achieve this, the first step is understanding the core drivers of those with whom we communicate on an individual basis. This forms the foundation for meaningful guidance.

The five love languages and the six human needs are my primary tools for adapting to meet an individual's personal needs. I promise that when you study these two powerful tools, you will not only elevate your mentoring and communication to another level, but you will also increase your ability to empathize and connect with individuals on a much deeper level.

Understanding The 'Six Human Needs'

Understanding 'The Six Human Needs' by Tony Robbins and applying them as a mentor in a child's life can significantly contribute to deep understanding as they development. Here's a brief guide:

1. **Certainty:**
   - Acknowledge the child's need for stability. Establish a consistent and reliable presence in their life.
   - Provide a structured environment while allowing room for flexibility and growth.

2. **Uncertainty/Variety:**
   - Foster adaptability by exposing the child to diverse experiences and challenges.
   - Encourage them to explore new interests, promoting creativity and a sense of excitement.

3. **Significance:**
   - Recognize and celebrate the child's achievements, no matter how small, to fulfill their need for importance.
   - Encourage them to set personal goals and support them in achieving these milestones.

4. **Love/Connection:**
   - Build a strong emotional connection by actively listening, showing genuine care and spending quality time together.
   - Create a supportive and inclusive environment to fulfill their need for love and belonging.

5. Growth:
- Cultivate a growth mindset by praising effort, resilience and a passion for learning.
- Support the child's personal development by helping them set and achieve meaningful goals.

6. Contribution:
- Instill a sense of empathy and responsibility by involving the child in acts of kindness and community service.
- Teach the importance of making a positive impact on others' lives, fostering a sense of purpose.

How to Be Aware of These Needs as a Mentor:
- Active Observation: Pay close attention to the child's behavior, noting any patterns or changes that may indicate unmet needs.
- Open Communication: Create a safe space for the child to express their feelings, desires, and experiences openly.
- Encourage Reflection: Prompt the child to reflect on their goals, values, and the impact of their actions on others.
- Adapt a Mentoring Approach: Tailor your mentoring style based on the child's evolving needs, striking a balance between guidance and autonomy.

By understanding and addressing these six human needs as a mentor, you can contribute significantly to the child's emotional well-being, personal growth and overall life satisfaction.

Understanding the Concept of the Five Love Languages for Children

Understanding a child's primary love language enhances the parent/mentor-child relationship, ensuring that expressions of love and connection are received and acknowledged in a way that resonates with the child. It's important to note that children may have a combination of these love languages, but identifying their primary one guides parents/mentors in providing the most effective expressions of love and support.

Introduced by Dr. Gary Chapman and Dr. Ross Campbell, this concept is rooted in the idea that individuals express and receive love and connection in varied ways, assisting parents/mentors in effectively communicating love and connection to their children.

1. Words of Affirmation:
Verbal expressions of love and encouragement, such as saying "I appreciate you" or "I love you" or offering specific compliments on their efforts and achievements, resonate well with some children, making them feel valued.

2. Acts of Service:
Actions speak louder than words for some children. They feel loved and connected when parents/mentors engage in tasks for them, whether it's helping with homework, preparing a special meal, or assisting with important activities.

3. Gifts:

This love language involves expressing love and connection through thoughtful gifts. It doesn't require extravagant presents; even small, meaningful tokens can make a child feel loved and appreciated.

4. Quality Time:

Children with this love language value spending quality time with their parents/mentors. Meaningful interactions, focused attention, and shared activities contribute to them feeling connected and loved.

5. Physical Touch:

Physical affection serves as the primary love language for some children. Hugs, kisses, pats on the back, or any form of physical contact reassure them of love and security.

EMPOWER AWARENESS

RECOGNIZING MANIPULATION AND FUNDAMENTAL DISCIPLINE STRATEGIES

- Six forms of manipulation and testing
- Who is training whom?
- Essential Guidelines for Effective Discipline

Six Forms of Manipulation and Testing

Every time I explain the six forms of manipulation to a parent in detail, they immediately think of their child and how they use one of these tactics to get what they want. The key is to create awareness and understand that these behaviors are most often present to achieve their desires. When we adhere to their behaviors, we are now the ones who are becoming trained, much like Pavlov's dog.

Here are the six forms of manipulation and testing:

Children often resort to testing and manipulation to get what they want, whether it's avoiding bedtime, craving candy before dinner, resisting school, or just wanting attention. They typically employ six tactics:

1. Badgering: Persistent pleas and repetition to wear you down.
2. Intimidation: Aggressive verbal attacks or tantrums, including yelling or accusations.
3. Threats: Promising negative consequences unless demands are met.
4. Martyrdom: Silent treatment, refusal to eat, or expressions of sadness to induce guilt.
5. Butterup: Complimenting or behaving well to achieve a goal.
6. Physical: Resorting to physical aggression, breaking things, or running away.

Parents often encounter challenges in handling these tactics, such as trying to find the right words or reasons to make the child quiet. Giving in to the child's demands may stop immediate testing, but it raises the question of who is in control. Buttering up, where a child tries to make you feel good, can be tricky to distinguish from genuine affection. Physical tactics become scarier as children grow.

Research indicates that badgering, intimidation, and martyrdom are the most common tactics. Girls tend to use Martyrdom more, while boys favor Intimidation. Successful testing efforts lead to prolonged emotional upsets in the household, damaging everyone's self-esteem in the long run.

Now that we've become aware of these tactics, it is imperative that we take action. My ultimate goal is to catch these behaviors in the moment and make sure that we are calling attention to it. I also let the child know that martyrdom, badgering, threatening, whining, anger and sweet talk are not appropriate.

I am a big fan of 123 magic (a method of counting before timeouts) but the ultimate rule is whatever form of discipline you use you must follow through and be consistent. There should be no idle threats. Lastly, understand that they will mirror your behaviors. If you discipline them with anger, threatening, bartering or physical tactics, they will begin to learn that is the way we solve problems.

Who is training whom?

If a child attends an afterschool event and throws a tantrum, expressing dislike for the gymnastic class that day, responding by taking them home, letting them have cookies, and watching Paw Patrol reinforces their belief that complaining leads to rewards. In times like this, it is imperative that we stand our ground. It is important for us to be patient and avoid negotiating with these threats. We need to listen to them and guide their behavior positively while respectfully standing our ground. This may be counterintuitive to our nature in rescuing our children in times of need, but we must realize that often we can do more harm than good if we are giving in to their manipulative tactics as they now become the ones conditioning us. While standing our ground, make sure that we continue to do our best to use positive reinforcement, and after working through these challenging situations disguised as a struggle for control, encourage resilience by praising their toughness and ability to make it through a tough day. Use the powerful tool of anchoring and remind our children when they make it through these challenging tasks that they should be very proud of themselves for making it through the afterschool event on a challenging day. Not crying when they fell down. Being brave when they went to the doctor, etc. I make a point to foster a mindset that values resilience over seeking attention through martyrdom, threats, complaining, or even sweet talk. At the end of the day, we have to create awareness around the fact that in these challenging situations, somebody is always training somebody.

Do:

1. Practice patience and positive reinforcement.
2. Avoid negotiating with treats for routine tasks.
3. Encourage resilience and toughness in challenging situations.

Don't:

1. Reward tantrums with treats and privileges.
2. Reinforce attention-seeking behaviors during minor setbacks.
3. Overindulge in immediate comfort for every complaint or discomfort.

Mentors, please remember that children are masters of manipulation. They know us better than anybody else and know how to get what they want. We must be consistent and resilient, keeping in mind that if we break first, we are the ones being trained.

Essential Guidelines for Effective Discipline

Always follow through and ensure you maintain consistency. These are the two key points. Making idle threats and being inconsistent will completely break down the legitimacy of your parenting authority. Stay strong and lead with love and empathy. First, always try to focus on positive reinforcement, but understand that structure and discipline are your responsibility.

Do's and Don'ts for Effective Discipline:

Do: Maintain a Calm and Consistent Approach
- Stay composed to help children understand the seriousness of their actions.

Don't: Resort to Violence or Anger
- Avoid resorting to violence or anger; seek alternative strategies to address challenging behaviors.

Do: Clearly Communicate Expectations
- Ensure children understand the connection between behavior and outcomes through clear communication of expectations and consequences.

Do: Tailor Consequences to Developmental Stage
- Make consequences meaningful and understandable based on a child's developmental stage.

Don't: Use Overly Harsh or Lenient Response

> Steer clear of consequences that are overly harsh or lenient. "Do: Ensure Fairness and Proportionality Keep consequences fair and proportionate.

Do: Ensure Fairness and Proportionality

> Keep consequences fair and proportionate, avoiding overly harsh or lenient responses.

Don't: Neglect Immediate Feedback

> Don't delay providing feedback; connect consequences promptly with behavior to reinforce the cause-and-effect relationship.

Do: Balance with Positive Reinforcement

> Acknowledge and reward positive actions, maintaining a balance with consequences for good behavior.

Don't: Ignore Positive Reinforcement

> Don't overlook positive reinforcement; acknowledge and reward positive actions to encourage repetition.

Do: Involve Children in Decision-Making

> Foster a cooperative approach by involving children in discussions about rules and consequences, encouraging a sense of responsibility.

Don't: Exclude Children from Decision-Making

> Avoid excluding children from discussions about rules and consequences; involve them to encourage a sense of responsibility.

Do: Teach Problem-Solving Skills

> Empower children to make better choices by helping them understand the impact of their actions which reinforces problem-solving skills.

Don't: Disregard Teaching Problem-Solving Skills

>> Don't disregard the importance of teaching problem-solving skills; empower children to make better choices.

Do: Parental Adaptability for Behavior Change

>> Be willing to adapt your approach, create new consequences, and commit to consistency for positive behavior changes.

Remember, these guidelines provide a balanced approach to effective discipline, ensuring a positive and constructive environment for your child's development.

FUNDAMENTAL COMMUNICATION STRATEGIES

- It isn't what they say about you; it's what they whisper
- What is praise-correct-praise?
- Coaching in the wanted behavior
- Catching your child being good
- Praising Children for Effort Over Ability
- Leading with empathy
- Audio, visual, kinesthetic
- Memorable Communication

It isn't what they say about you it's what they whisper

It's not about what they openly say, but the power lies in their whispers – a force that often conveys true feelings. Recognizing this, we can strategically leverage it in child development by focusing on two key aspects. First, by effectively conveying a message and capturing a child's attention. Next, by shaping their identity.

Consider two scenarios: In the first, parents discuss a child's grades on the couch, expressing concerns about ADD, trouble focusing, and being a less-than-ideal listener, implying that something might be wrong. In the second scenario, we harness this to our advantage by consciously shaping the narrative. Here, parents highlight the child's perseverance, recounting instances where they didn't give up on challenges. This anticipation of their resilience becomes a source of excitement for the upcoming school term.

In my discussions, I often emphasize the 'power of I am.' Just as what follows "I am" shapes our identity, the same principle applies to what we say about our children. The phrases "He is, She is, We are" prove to be powerful in shaping a child's identity.

Being mindful of these identity whispers and intentionally planting them can be a proactive step in purposefully developing a child's character.

The second strength of the whisper lies in its ability to captivate a child's attention. In moments of high stress, while striving to meet Maslow's needs, parents tend to issue direct commands and expect swift compliance. However, there's immense power in communication through a whisper.

Gently settling your little one with a patient whisper becomes a soothing mist, saturating them with unconditional love and support, preventing hidden rage from erupting. Always remember, regardless of the problem, kindness is the most fitting response.

How to Use:

1. Craft Positive Narratives:

- Choose Encouraging Stories: Share anecdotes that highlight your child's perseverance and resilience during challenges.
- Emphasize Growth: Whisper about their growth, focusing on instances where they overcame difficulties, creating excitement about their potential.

2. **Utilize Affirmative Language:**
    - » Be Intentional with "I am": Use affirming phrases starting with "I am," "He is," or "We are" to positively influence your child's self-perception.
    - » Highlight Strengths: Whisper about their strengths and positive qualities, reinforcing a strong and positive identity.

3. **Be Mindful of Words:**
    - » Reflect Before Whispering: Consider the impact your words might have on your child's self-image before speaking.
    - » Choose Uplifting Language: Opt for words that uplift and encourage, avoiding negative labels that could affect their confidence.

4. **Effective Communication in Stressful Moments:**
    - » Whisper Love and Support: During moments of stress, communicate through whispers to provide comfort, love, and support.
    - » Create a Soothing Atmosphere: Use patient whispers as a calming presence, preventing hidden rage and promoting a sense of security.

Remember, the effectiveness of whispers lies in their positivity and intent, contributing to the holistic development of your child.

What Is Praise-Correct-Praise?

Here are some examples of a direct correction that does not employ the praise-correct-praise method.

1. "This is all wrong. What were you thinking? You need to redo it, and this time, try not to make such a mess."
2. "Your creativity here is off track. There's a lot to fix. Be more careful, and maybe you'll get it right next time."
3. "This is far from good. Are you even trying? Fix it, and maybe, just maybe, you'll start doing okay."

Here are examples following the praise-correct-praise pattern:

1. "Great attempt at solving the problem! Let's refine the approach a bit. Awesome job for taking on the challenge!"
2. "I love your creativity in handling this task. There's a small adjustment needed. Keep up the fantastic effort and willingness to learn!"
3. "You're doing well with this task. A tiny tweak will make it even better. I appreciate your hard work and positive attitude!"

Envision a scenario where, each time you made a mistake, I responded by smacking you upside your head. Following the initial incident, you might instinctively raise your hands. Subsequently, you could develop a tendency to shy away. If this pattern persists and your natural defense mechanisms activate, you may opt to avoid me entirely or even engage in confrontation. When children associate correction with pain, they often learn to tune out that discomfort by seeking a mental safe space or, regrettably, nurturing revenge fantasies. When mentors are not skilled in praise, correct praise, and tend to deliver corrections harshly, they are training children to be on the defense much like the examples above. Recognizing the potency of words, our mindful communication of PCP with our children not only enhances their receptivity to messages but also instills in them the ability to express themselves effectively. With over 30 years of teaching experience, I've encountered children facing challenges like those grappling with social skills and difficulty conveying messages kindly. They typically draw influence from external sources like family members, friends, television shows, Instagram, etc. As parents or mentors, we wield substantial influence as mirrors to these young minds. Thus, a conscientious effort in our communication style not only fosters greater responsiveness to corrections but also imparts valuable communication skills to our children.

Coaching in the Wanted Behavior

In parenting and coaching, being aware of both our children's actions and our own is key. Just as we notice what they're doing, we need to consciously nurture the behaviors we want to see, essentially choosing which "wolf" to feed.

"The habits you praise become the child you raise" underscores the importance of shifting our language and actions to encourage positive behaviors. Imagine teaching a child to ride a bike—instead of saying "Don't hit that tree," we can use phrases like "Keep your eyes forward, stay focused, maintain strong arms." Positive reinforcement, like saying "Thank you for being such a tough boy/girl," works better than language focusing on potential negatives. Avoiding phrases like "don't cry" or "don't be afraid" helps guide their thoughts in a positive direction.

Balancing negative and positive language is crucial. Excessive negative words can stress a child's brain. Opt for positive framing, such as "Let's explore different solutions together," instead of creating unnecessary pressure with phrases like "Failure is not an option." Clear positives enhance understanding, promoting self-awareness and celebrating good behaviors.

In coaching, use negative words strategically to maintain motivation. As a director of attention, choose words guiding toward goals. Introduce the 5:1 ratio to kids—counteracting one negative with five positives—fostering optimism and positive relationships for a supportive environment.

Do examples:

1. Positive Bike Riding Coaching:

- » Guide Positively: When teaching bike riding, use phrases like "Keep your eyes forward, stay focused, maintain strong arms" instead of focusing on what not to do.
- » Express Gratitude: Reinforce positive behaviors by saying "Thank you for being such a tough boy/girl," emphasizing strengths over potential negatives.

2. Fostering Positive Mindset:

- » Avoid Negative Phrases: Refrain from saying "don't cry" or "don't be afraid," steering thoughts positively.
- » Use Positive Framing: Encourage positive thinking with phrases like "Let's explore different solutions together" instead of creating unnecessary pressure with " Why do you keep messing up?"

Don't examples:

1. Excessive Negative Words:

- ❯ Avoid Overusing Negatives: Refrain from using too many negative words, as this can stress a child's brain and hinder their development.
- ❯ Strive for Balance: Incorporate positive language to create a balanced approach, enhancing understanding and promoting self-awareness.

2. Unsupportive Language:

- ❯ Steer Clear of Unnecessary Pressure: Avoid phrases like "Failure is not an option," which may create fear instead of encouragement.
- ❯ Focus on Positives: Celebrate good behaviors and foster a supportive atmosphere by focusing on clear positives rather than highlighting potential failures.

Catching Your Child Being Good

As a parent or mentor, we often find ourselves going about our everyday lives and only stepping in when things go wrong. The biggest challenge with this is that we are conditioning our children to expect attention only when they misbehave. Once we begin to make a conscious effort to catch our child being good, it will eventually become an unconscious act, feeding our child's positive behaviors and self-esteem.

Catching your child being good is important because giving positive attention for good behavior teaches them which behaviors you like and encourages them to continue those positive actions.

What You Will Need:

- Small rewards based on the five love languages, such as quality time (a favorite activity together), words of affirmation (praising their effort), acts of service (helping with a task), receiving gifts (small tokens), or physical touch (a hug or high five).

Refer to the five love languages for rewards and use AVK (Audio, Visual, Kinesthetic) for communication.

What to Do:

- At first, try to catch your child being good randomly, or at least once every 15 minutes.
- Make eye contact.
- Speak with excitement.
- Be specific about the behavior you like, such as saying, "I love how you asked for a drink of water," or "You did a great job picking up all of your toys."
- Give attention right after the behavior you liked. Avoid giving attention immediately after a behavior you did NOT like. Ensure your child exhibits positive behavior for at least 30 seconds before receiving attention.
- Provide the type of attention your child enjoys. If your child does not like kisses, then give a hug or a high five instead.
- Give positive attention for even small improvements. For example, say, "That was great throwing your trash away," or "You did a nice job walking into the store today."
- Identify behaviors that cannot occur simultaneously. For instance, instead of punching their sibling, they could use Play-Doh® or speak quietly instead of screaming or whining.

Celebrating Overlooked Good Behavior:
- ❯ Typical Good Behavior: Acknowledging and praising your child when they independently share a toy with a friend without being prompted.
- ❯ What to Do: Make eye contact, speak with excitement, and be specific about the behavior you appreciate. For instance, say, "I love how you shared your toy with your friend." Reinforce this positive behavior with attention and encouragement.

Overemphasized Everyday Martyrdom:
- ❯ Typical Everyday Behavior: Giving excessive attention when a child acts as a "martyr," showcasing negative behaviors to gain sympathy or special treatment.
- ❯ What to Avoid: Instead of reinforcing martyrdom, redirect their attention towards positive actions. Wait until your child exhibits positive behavior for at least 30 seconds before providing attention and praise. Encourage and celebrate behaviors that promote cooperation and kindness rather than emphasizing negative actions seeking sympathy.

Praising Children for Effort Over Ability

When acknowledging your child's achievements, emphasize their effort instead of innate abilities. If children think their skills are innate, they may invest less effort—practicing, studying, and trying less.

Rather than praising inherent talent, focus on acknowledging the effort students exert to reach their goals, as praise plays a crucial role in motivating and inspiring children.

Avoiding Failure

Excessive praise can backfire. Constantly praising something beyond a child's control can lead to a sense of powerlessness, making it challenging to handle failure and damaging self-confidence. Instead of saying, "you are so smart," opt for "you worked really hard. Awesome job!"

Research on Success & Failure

In a study with 5th graders, psychologists praised some for intelligence and others for hard work. Faced with a setback, those praised for effort were more resilient, taking the test home to practice.

Two Mindsets

Research shows differentiates between fixed and growth mindsets. A fixed mindset believes in innate talents, while a growth mindset values persistence, effort, determination, and practice.

Effective Effort Praise Ideas:

- » Praise Process, Not Outcome: Commend students for hard work and dedication, linking their effort to results. When celebrating a good mark, say, "you deserve it! You worked really hard for that." Praise the entire process, including concentration, self-correction, and strategies used.
- » Praise Specifically and Sincerely: Children appreciate attention and feedback, but insincere praise is noticeable. Be specific to make the praise meaningful, acknowledging their efforts genuinely.

Praising for Success

Praising effort over innate skills helps students understand the connection between work and desired results. Skills like perseverance and dedication enable them to take risks, learn from mistakes, and move forward from setbacks.

Effort Over Ability:

- » Instead of saying, "You're so smart," say, "I appreciate how hard you worked on understanding that problem."
- » Instead of praising talent, say, "Your dedication and effort in practicing the piano really show."

- Instead of focusing on innate skills, acknowledge their perseverance by stating, "I'm proud of the effort you put into your school project."

Highlighting Process and Improvement:
- Instead of emphasizing natural abilities, recognize their improvement with phrases like, "I can see how much you've progressed in your artwork with consistent practice."
- Instead of focusing on inherent talent, shift the focus to their effort by saying, "Your commitment to learning new things is impressive."
- Encourage a growth mindset by acknowledging effort in the face of challenges by saying "I admire how you talked that difficult program by persisting and trying different approaches."

Leading with Empathy

Mentoring comes with its own set of challenges, especially when guiding children who learn and think differently. It's crucial to be aware of the "Little Adult Assumption," which assumes that children are naturally reasonable and cooperative, akin to miniature adults. This belief can lead to the counterproductive "Talk-Persuade-Argue-Yell-Hit Syndrome" when addressing a child's undesirable behavior. Despite good intentions, this approach may escalate conflicts, contribute to child abuse, and inadvertently encourage defiance.

Why is this important to know? Empathy plays a vital role in navigating these challenges. It's more than just understanding feelings; it's a superpower that strengthens the bond between you and your child, creating a supportive space tailored to their unique needs. As we delve into this guide, let's explore the art of empathetic communication. It's not just about words; it's about building strong and lasting connections with our kids.

Step-by-Step Guide to Expressing Empathy to Kids: An Example Situation:

1. Identify the Situation:
- ❯❯ Your child struggles to get ready for school, causing frustration for both of you.

2. Recognize Your Emotions:
- ❯❯ Understandably, you feel stressed about being consistently late.

3. **Shift Focus to Your Child:**
   - Instead of solely focusing on your feelings, redirect your attention to what your child is experiencing.

4. **Initiate Empathetic Response:**
   - Begin by acknowledging your child's feelings. "I see that getting ready for school has been challenging for you."

5. **Express Understanding:**
   - Emphasize your understanding of their frustration. "I can imagine it's frustrating to feel rushed every morning."

6. **Highlight Shared Feelings:**
   - Connect with your child by expressing that you, too, would feel upset in a similar situation. "I'd be upset too if I had to hurry every day."

7. **Introduce Empathy Elements:**
   - Explain the four main elements of empathy:
   - Taking Perspective: Encourage yourself to see the situation through your child's eyes. Ask, "Do I believe my child is trying their best?"
   - Putting Aside Judgment: Take a step back before forming conclusions. Ask, "What more do I need to know about what's going on with my child?"
   - Understanding Feelings: Tap into your experiences to comprehend your child's feelings. Ask, "What else do I need to learn about how my child is seeing or reacting to this situation?"
   - Communicating Understanding: Let your child express their feelings without immediately offering solutions. Use reflective phrases like "It sounds like you..." or "I hear that you..."

8. **Clarify Empathy vs. Sympathy:**
   - Distinguish between empathy and sympathy. Emphasize that empathy doesn't require lowering expectations but validates your child's feelings while maintaining high standards.

9. **Highlight the Importance of Self-Awareness:**
   - Explain that tuning into your child's emotions not only shows understanding but also fosters self-awareness and the ability to articulate their needs.

10. **Encourage Practice:**
    - Acknowledge that responding with empathy takes practice. Try role-playing with a partner or recording yourself to help further develop empathetic communication skills.

11. **Emphasize the End Goal:**
    - Remind yourself that the ultimate goal is to communicate in a way that resonates with your child, fostering a connection built on understanding and support.

12. **Summarize Key Takeaways:**
    - Recap the key points: Empathy isn't about feeling sorry; it's about sincerely telling your child, "You're not alone, and I want to understand how this feels to you."

Situation 1: Inappropriate Language

Child: Using bad language.

Mentor: Maintain a serious tone and facial expression. "Excuse me, I wouldn't mind if you refrained from using inappropriate language. It's not the way we express ourselves here. Can you tell me a better way to communicate your feelings without using those words?"

Follow up with a conversation emphasizing the impact of respectful communication and the importance of expressing oneself without offensive language.

Situation 2: Running in a Dangerous Area

Child: Running in a potentially unsafe area.

Mentor: Approach with a serious demeanor. "Excuse me, I appreciate your energy, but running in this area is not safe. Can you think of a better place to run and play? Let's talk about why this location might not be suitable."

Continue by discussing safety concerns, potential consequences, and guiding the child towards making better choices while using respectful language throughout the interaction.

Audio, Visual, Kinesthetic: The Three Primary Ways People Absorb Information

First, it's crucial to understand that people learn in three primary ways: auditory, visual, and kinesthetic. When interacting with a group, my ultimate goal is for them to absorb the provided information, so I consciously employ all three learning tools.

Typically, I teach with a whiteboard behind me to emphasize major points. For instance, if the topic is focus, I would write it on the board. For kinesthetic and auditory learners, I engage them by having them repeat phrases like, "When I am focused, nothing can stop me," pointing to their eyes as they do so. Here, I have covered visual with the whiteboard, acted it out for auditory and kinesthetic learners, and once again, emphasized visual as we point to our eyes.

When communicating with my children, I often kneel down, convey important messages through stories, and encourage them to repeat. For instance, if I find my child blindly throwing a rock over a fence, instead of a direct order to stop, I approach the child, take a knee, and ask, "Excuse me, is that appropriate?" while gently touching the lower part of their chin. I then pose questions like, "What could happen if we hit somebody? Could they get hurt?" Following their response, I share a personal story about being hit by a rock as a young boy, highlighting the consequences.

To enhance engagement, I employ physical touch, prompting discussions about where and why we throw rocks. This approach incorporates audiovisual and kinesthetic learning, ensuring active participation and a meaningful connection to the lesson.

Engage visual learners by using diagrams, charts and pictures, and animated gestures.

Engage auditory learners by stressing key words, using call to response, and telling stories and anecdotes.

Engage kinesthetic learners by including physical activities and "hands-on" tasks and appropriate physical touch.

- Visual: learners respond to images and graphics.
- Auditory: learners prefer verbal presentations.
- Kinesthetic: learners prefer a physical, hands-on approach.

Memorable Communication

Locking information into the memory with two great teaching tools

#1 Memorable Cues

Creating memorable metaphors or analogies enhances communication and aids memorization.

Scenario 1 - Learning in an Exercise Setting:

- ›› Child: Performs exercises with loud stomping.
- ›› Mentor: Your strength is impressive! Let's move quietly and gracefully, landing as softly as a whispering breeze. Can you show me how to perform the exercise with a gentle touch?

Scenario 2 - School Setting:

- ›› Child: Runs into the classroom.
- ›› Mentor: I appreciate your enthusiasm, but let's enter the classroom like graceful butterflies. Can you show me how butterflies enter?

Scenario 3 - Behaviors in Public:

- ›› Child: Loudly talks during a library visit.
- ›› Mentor: I love your stories, but in the library, we need to be as quiet as sleeping kittens. Can you show me how kittens talk quietly?

These scenarios use metaphors to help children understand and remember desired behaviors in different situations.

#2 The Power of Teaching in Threes

From one to a couple to a few, and then many... teaching in threes packs a punch. Forget The Four Musketeers; they stuck with D'Artagnan and the Three. ABCs? 1, 2, 3 – it's about the power of three.

Students often drown in too much information, excessive talk, and numerous tasks. With over 30 years of experience teaching people of all ages, one of the greatest skills I've acquired is the power of three.

Below, I'll use one of the most effective analogies I know: striking. Please note that this is just an analogy and applies to all areas of life.

Here's an example of breaking down a nine-hitbox combination, which can be incredibly challenging before beginning. For instance, consider jab-cross-hook, cross-hook-cross, and uppercut-hook-cross.

Teaching it in threes makes it very palatable:

1. Jab-cross-hook
2. Cross-hook-cross
3. Uppercut-hook-cross

Chunking this combination into threes is easy and memorable. Attempting to teach a nine-step combo all at once is particularly challenging for someone just beginning.

Apply this concept to all things in life; less is more, and three is the maximum. If we wish to hyperfocus on technique, we can break it down even further and chunk down a simple technique like punching:

- Chin down
- Elbow tight
- Twist your wrist

Remember, this can be applied to all things in life and all scenarios. The simpler we keep it, the more memorable it will be. Our rule is never to go over three. It is even more effective if you can give one or two powerful things to focus on (for example, coaching an athlete between rounds I recommend one, maximum two coaching tips in this scenario). But when teaching something in a large pattern, we always chunk it down to three.

EMOTIONAL GUIDANCE

> Addressing the Fight or Flight Response in Children
> Transforming Anger
> ANTs — Automatic Negative Thoughts
> A Process for Transforming a Negative Belief

Addressing the Fight or Flight Response in Children

Imagine a typical day as you prepare to go shopping with your child at Target. As you enter the store, you notice that the usual race car shopping carts are all taken. In this moment, your child insists on having the race car shopping cart and proceeds to fall over, as if it's the end of the world. What unfolds at this precise moment holds significance—your child has experienced a surge of hormones, throwing them off balance. They've completely transitioned into their emotional brain, and logic has taken a back seat. The key lies in knowing how to navigate this moment swiftly, understanding that missteps can inadvertently reinforce undesired behaviors.

Understanding and managing emotional hijacking, or the shutdown of the amygdala, is crucial for navigating stress and maintaining emotional well-being. The amygdala, a part of the brain associated with emotions, triggers a fight-or-flight response during moments of stress, occasionally overwhelming logical thinking. Recognizing and addressing these emotional hijacks is especially vital when dealing with children, significantly impacting their ability to navigate challenges effectively.

Dealing with Emotional Hijacking

When confronted with an emotional hijack, it's crucial to realize that the symptoms stem from the body's chemical response to stress. For children, their fight-or-flight response has been triggered, and it typically takes 18-22 minutes for it to subside. In this critical moment, our actions matter. Despite the deep-rooted nature of the fight-or-flight response, it is possible to regain control.

Here are four practical brain hacks to pause overwhelming emotions and restore a state of logic and reasoning:

Hack #1 - Name the Emotion

Simply recognizing and naming the experienced emotion can shift the focus back to rational thinking. For example, acknowledging, "I feel so mad," facilitates a transition to a more reasoned mindset. Make sure they use the phrase "I feel" instead of "I am," noting to the child that "this is just a feeling," not who you are.

Hack #2 - Change the Setting

Similar to naming emotions, changing the physical setting by moving around automatically prompts consideration of one's surroundings. This reactivates the thinking parts of the brain that may have been temporarily shut down.

Hack #3 - Do a Quick Math Problem

Engaging in a simple cognitive task, like counting, solving a math problem, or recognizing colors, jumpstarts rational thinking and aids in shifting the mental state from emotional to logical.

Hack #4 - Share the Mental Load

Drawing from a study on social support, sharing the emotional burden with another person can make challenges seem less daunting. Similarly, sharing the mental load with a child helps them feel less threatened and facilitates a collaborative approach to managing emotions.

Dealing with Emotional Hijacking in Real Life

Here is a quick step-by-step guide on how to handle children who experience emotional hijack when being dropped off at a class. First, set your child up for success by ensuring all of Maslow's needs are met. Make sure they are fed, hydrated, etc. Do your best to avoid rushing; give yourself a buffer. For example, don't wait until the last minute to put their clothing on in the car if possible.

When the child has a meltdown, understand that somebody is always training somebody. With this mantra, repeat: remember to stay calm and resilient. Typically, I ask parents to leave because these children have become masters at manipulating their parents, knowing just the right button to push to get what they want.

Immediately, I try to change their state by becoming level and open, offering a high five, and often playing the game where I pull it away and say "too slow." Hopefully, this changes their state and makes them laugh. If they hit me, I pretend like it hurt tremendously. If they are still shut down or hiding, I continue to try and engage. My goal is to shift them from their emotional brain to their logical brain, getting them to have a conversation. I begin by asking questions, for example, pointing to their belt and asking what color it is or how many stripes it has.

If they have three stripes, I ask how many they have left to get to five. If I can get them in that position, we have opened the door, and I continue with this approach until we can start a conversation. I might do something silly, like having them hit a paddle and making it fly away, to further change their emotional state. The goal is to learn how to shift their thinking, but sometimes there is a point of diminishing returns, and at that moment, we must recognize that they need time.

Please note, this time is unwavering. If a student is having a meltdown and doesn't want to enter class, I tell the parents to be patient. The worst thing they can do is go home, sit on the couch, eat cookies, and watch Paw Patrol. In doing so, they are inadvertently training their child that meltdowns equal rewards. Instead, sit with your child, or in this case, leave your child with the instructors and we will address it. Remember, somebody is always training somebody, and it's imperative to stay resilient.

Transforming Anger

The realization we should all embrace is about reshaping how we understand emotions, particularly when it comes to dealing with anger. We need to acknowledge that anger often comes from feeling limited in our choices. Similar to sadness, anger is a signal that nudges us to explore other solutions, framing it as a kind of ignorance that we can collectively address. When anger shows up, it's like an open invitation for us to explore what we all might not know and the alternative options we might be missing. This shift, if we adopt it, can turn learning into a remedy we share. Anger can be an opportunity for our joint growth which can help eliminate the need for anyone to hold on to this emotion. The quote "Become wise or become wounded" echoes the power of gaining knowledge and offers various ways to enlighten ourselves and collaboratively navigate challenges-anger management included.

"Holding on to anger is like grasping a hot coal with the intent of throwing it at someone else; you are the one who gets burned."

In the ups and downs of feelings, anger can be a tough one to navigate. Here are three simple tips for giving advice on anger:

1. Forgive Them:

- When anger hits, think about forgiving. If you truly forgive someone, and I mean truly forgive them, you cannot be angry at them. Saying "I forgive you wholeheartedly" means you have let go. Letting go of grudges is a gift to yourself. Forgiveness creates room for healing and brings peace.

2. Forgive Ourselves:

- If pride, ego, or circumstance does not allow you to forgive the person, forgive yourself for letting it bother you. We are all human and learning to forgive ourselves will help us grow stronger. By forgiving yourself instead of the other person, you leave it completely in your power.

3. Pity Them:

- Once again, pride, ego, or situation may prevent you from forgiving them or forgiving yourself. If that's the case, the next step is to feel sorry or pity them. If you truly feel sorry for someone or pity them, it is very difficult to be angry at them. Show understanding for those causing anger. Maybe they're facing challenges. Encourage empathy instead of judging, and it'll lead to better connections.

These tips aren't just for anger. They are tools to help guide you to feeling good and building better relationships.

ANTs — Automatic Negative Thoughts

ANTS or Automatic Negative Thoughts, are negative thinking patterns that can cause stress. It's important to be aware of them because recognizing and challenging these thoughts helps promote a positive mindset, reduce anxiety, and improve mental health. Being aware of these pesky ANTS empowers people to replace negative thoughts with more constructive ones, supporting emotional well-being as well as a growth mindset.

The ability to shift our perspective is a superpower. Transforming something as simple as anxiety into excitement empowers us. For example, understanding how to shift our mindset and educate ourselves on any subject is the key to overcoming most mental challenges. Either educating ourselves or shifting our perspective can once again change our emotions and beliefs.

Here's a process I used with kids to identify and hopefully gain control over automatic negative thoughts (also referred to as an aversion of anxiety). "When people get into a negative state of mind, it's easy to remember all the bad things someone said or did to you, and hard to remember your successes."

Imagine there is a talking ant on your shoulder. This ant tells you things like "you look stupid," "everyone is going to be upset with you," or "you're not good enough." Whenever these thoughts pop into your head, imagine the ant on your shoulder and talk back. Say that it's not true and repeat the opposite. For example, if the ant says, "you're not good enough," respond with "that's not true; I am awesome." Pantomime and imagine smashing that that talking bug on your shoulder and stomp on it for good measure.

Another effective version is to write down the negative thought, think of creative ways to destroy it, then write down the new belief/replacement. Frame it, mail it, decorate it, etc. Creating these powerful before-and-after moments can be impactful.

Drill 1: Ant Visualization

- » Close your eyes and imagine a talking ant on your shoulder feeding negative thoughts.
- » Challenge the ant by verbalizing positive statements and physically pantomime smashing the bug and stomping on it.

Drill 2: Thought Transformation Exercise

- » Identify a recurring negative thought and write it down.
- » Devise creative ways to destroy this thought, then write down a positive belief as a replacement.
- » Frame, mail, or decorate this transformed belief, creating a tangible reminder of your ability to conquer automatic negative thoughts.

A Process for Transforming a Negative Belief

Imagine the ability to pull a child out of negative self beliefs, such as fear of failure, doubts about personal abilities, or thoughts of not being good enough.

A belief is an absolute certainty, that something is true. This process gets a person to question their belief, then gets our foot in the door, to prove the point and shift their perspective into a more positive light.

Here Is an extremely successful process to help shift someone out of the negative belief.

Story:

Child: I don't have any friends, and nobody likes me.

Mentor: I understand that sometimes it feels like that. Let me ask you a question: Do I like you?

Child: Yes.

Mentor: Does your mother like you?

Child: Yes.

Mentor: I know that Lukas from your class likes you. He just wrote you a card for your birthday. Is that true?

Child: Yes.

Mentor: So let me ask you a question: Would you write a card for someone you didn't like?

Child: No, I wouldn't.

Mentor: So is it possible that maybe some people do actually like you?

Child: Oh yeah, I guess so.

Mentor: Just like making friends. Instead of saying "nobody likes me," remember, you are not only liked but loved. Repeat after me: "Only a few friends are for a lifetime; others will come and go."

Child: "Only a few friends are for a lifetime; others will come and go."

Mentor: Good job! Hand on your heart, say it again.

Child: "Only a few friends are for a lifetime; others will come and go."

Mentor: Now, repeat after me: "I am loved."

Child: "I am loved."

Mentor: One more time, please.

Child: "I am loved."

Mentor: Awesome! Whenever loneliness creeps in, remember this. Your heart knows you are loved. And you have some amazing lifetime friends, don't you?

Child: Yeah, I guess I do!

This is a powerful process that must be practiced. Once you have done it several times, you will begin to do it unconsciously, and it will become the go to pattern for dealing with these challenges.

Here's a step-by-step guide on how to help a child transform a negative belief:

1. Identify the negative belief: "I have no friends and nobody likes me."
2. Provide proof against the belief: Share instances where they've experienced kindness and friendship. For example, "Do you remover when Lukas wrote you a birthday card?" This highlights the connections the child has.
3. Reframe the belief: Encourage them to replace "nobody likes me" with "I haven't found all my friends yet." Repeat the positive affirmation, "Only a few friends are for a lifetime; others will come and go."
4. Anchor the new belief: Connect a specific action to the positive belief, like placing a hand on their heart while repeating the empowering statement.

By going through this process, a child can begin to question and reevaluate their belief, leading to a shift in their perception and emotional state. It can foster a more constructive and positive mindset.

SELF-FULFILLING PROPHECIES

- "We are the Type of People Who"
- The Impact of Tribe and Beliefs
- The Power of "I am"
- Attitude of Gratitude
- Power of Symbolism and Rituals

"We are the Type of People Who" The Impact of Tribe and Beliefs

Growing up, my father used to say, "You're a Graf, you're strong." These words became the foundation of my beliefs about what it means to be Graf. I not only embraced these beliefs but also reflected them in my actions. When mentoring, I harness the power of tribe, instilling in my children the understanding that Grafs are the kind of people who work hard, persevere, and never give up.

Teaching my students, I emphasize that we are the type of people who persevere and show kindness, compassion, empathy, and stand up to bullying. We are the type of people who never punched down and always make an effort to befriend, those sitting alone at a lunch table. The strength of "we are the type of people who" lies in its ability to shape our collective identity, fostering a sense of unity and shared values.

Believing profoundly in the influence of belonging to a tribe, we should recognize the tremendous power of the cultures we are a part of. Gangsters act like gangsters, frat boys act like frat boys. Their actions will be in alignment with who they identify as. Now it comes down to an awareness of choice. We can choose to join a supportive community that builds us up and helps us grow or if that's not an option, we can consciously decide not to engage in negative behaviors.

As parents and mentors, we hold control over our actions because the greatest outside influences in our children's lives will be their proximity, friends, and mentors. Knowing this, we strive to set our children up for success by creating a tribe where they can thrive, anchoring in the power of "we."

For instance, we declare that we are the type of people who, but the reality is, they will always follow our lead. It is imperative that if we desire positive outcomes for those we mentor, we must embody the principles we preach. The responsibility transcends us, recognizing that the power of "we" is key to achieving meaningful results. Make a conscious effort to create your tribe; your child's beliefs and community matter.

Action Items to Impact Tribe and Beliefs:

1. Embrace and Reinforce Identity Statements

- ❯ Continuously use identity statements like "We are the type of people who" to reinforce the positive traits and values associated with your tribe (e.g., Grafs).
- ❯ Encourage family members and tribe members to adopt and use these identity statements in their daily lives.

2. Incorporate Identity Statements in Daily Communication

- ❯ Regularly incorporate identity statements into conversations with your children, emphasizing values such as hard work, perseverance, and kindness.
- ❯ Integrate these statements into mentoring sessions, creating a consistent message for both family and mentees.

3. Extend Identity Statements to Education

- ❯ Work with educators and school administrators to integrate identity statements into the educational curriculum, fostering a sense of shared values among students.
- ❯ Encourage teachers to emphasize the positive qualities associated with your tribe, creating a supportive and cohesive environment.

4. Community Engagement

- ❯ Actively participate in community events and initiatives to contribute positively to the broader community.
- ❯ Organize or join community projects that align with the values you want to instill, reinforcing the positive impact your tribe can have.

5. Family Rituals and Traditions

- ❯ Establish family rituals and traditions that reflect the values expressed in identity statements.
- ❯ Ensure that family gatherings and celebrations incorporate discussions about the shared identity and values of your tribe.

6. Genetic Predisposition Narratives

- ❯ Develop narratives that emphasize positive traits as "genetically predisposed" in your family or tribe.

- Share stories and examples that highlight how these traits have been passed down through generations, creating a sense of continuity.

7. Cultural Understanding
- Encourage open discussions about cultural influences, recognizing that different groups may have distinct behaviors.
- Foster an environment of cultural understanding within your family and community to break stereotypes and promote unity.

8. Positive Role Modeling
- Demonstrate the values and behaviors you want to instill within your tribe through consistent positive actions.
- Serve as a role model for your children and mentees, showcasing the strength of your collective identity in action.

9. Community Inclusivity
- Actively seek to include and understand others in your community, promoting a sense of inclusivity.
- Engage in initiatives that bridge gaps between different communities, fostering a broader sense of unity.

10. Encourage Proximity with Positive Influences
- Facilitate interactions with positive role models, friends, and mentors who align with the values you wish to instill.
- Create opportunities for your children to be in proximity to individuals who positively contribute to the collective identity.

Remember, the impact of these actions is cumulative, and consistency is key to shaping a positive and influential tribe.

The Power of "I am"

The power of "I am" - Whatever you say after 'I am' is what you become

The power of mantra - "We become the phrases we repeatedly say."
Self-fulfilling prophecies - "What we believe, we become."

Understanding The Red Car Theory

Imagine cruising down the street, and all of a sudden, you spot a beautiful red car. Soon, everywhere you go, you begin to see red cars popping up. It's not about more cars on the road or that you may have manifested them; it's the simple fact that you have now created a heightened sense of awareness and focus regarding this stimulus. How do we apply this to kids and their development? Envision a child's environment, habits, and behaviors as these red cars. Have we trained their minds to see problems or solutions, pain or happiness, peace or stress? We believe that their words hold extreme power. If a child echoes a statement like "I can't do anything right," much like the red car, they will only be looking for their mistakes. On the contrary, if a child faces a challenge and uses simple affirmations like "I am capable of finding a solution," it will completely shift their focus towards positive beliefs. We are strong believers in the power of "I am," and that our personal focus are linked together. One of our favorite quotes to use when working with children is "where our focus goes, our energy flows," followed by whatever you say after "I am" is what you become. Understanding and empowering children with these statements can help shape their focus towards positive beliefs, fostering a mindset that recognizes opportunities. The theory's application to children, lies in the idea that early affirmations and positive self-talk will influence and aid in developing their positive mindset and reality.

Here is a guide on how to apply these superpowers to a child's everyday life. Applying any one of these consistently can make a tremendous impact.

Step 1: Introduce the Power of "I Am"

- Explain the profound nature of "I am" to the child, emphasizing its ability to shape their reality.

Step 2: Explore Self-Talk

- Encourage positive self-talk, highlighting the impact words can have on thoughts and feelings. Teach the child to replace self-limiting phrases with empowering ones.

Step 3: Create Personal Mantras

- Guide the child in crafting personal mantras reflecting their goals and aspirations.

Step 4: Understanding Self-Fulfilling Prophecies

- Explain self-fulfilling prophecies, helping them grasp that belief and positive speech can influence outcomes.

Step 5: Interactive Activities
- Engage the child in activities like journaling or role-playing to practice positive self-talk and recite their mantras.

Step 6: Consistent Reinforcement
- Regularly revisit the power of "I am," reinforcing the importance of words in shaping their reality.

Step 7: Encourage Reflection
- Promote self-reflection, celebrating instances where positive self-talk contributes to their achievements.

Step 8: Adapt and Grow
- As the child matures, discuss more complex aspects of self-identity and continual growth through mindful language use. Instill the understanding that their words are a powerful tool in creating the reality they desire.

Attitude of Gratitude

Studies show that if you express gratitude, it raises your happiness by 25%. So, these 10 simple ways to practice gratitude might just be the key to unlocking more joy in your life.

When mentoring children, we prompt the children to give 1 to 3 grateful statements, depending on the size of the group I'm working with. It's a powerful practice that sets a positive tone and encourages gratitude from an early age.

This drill brings into focus what we have versus what we don't have. If you are truly grateful for living in your house, it is challenging to be envious or ungrateful because somebody has a bigger house. Focusing on how grateful you are for the love of your family makes challenges seem out of sight, no matter what you're facing.

The little things. The little moments. They aren't little. Saying thank you, holding the door for someone – these little moments can change the tone of your whole day. One of the most powerful ways I've found to rewire my brain for more joy and less stress is to focus on gratitude.

Here are 10 action items to shift your state and get you focused on gratitude.

1. Keep a Gratitude Journal
- Set aside 5 minutes daily. In your journal, be explicit. Instead of "family," note "Mom's comforting words during a tough day" or "brother's surprise visit."

2. Remember the Bad
- Allocate 15 minutes weekly. Journal not only the challenging experience but also pinpoint two lessons learned and detail your personal growth since.

3. Ask Three Questions
- Find a quiet spot for 5-10 minutes. Ask yourself 3 questions which seek to bring your gratitude to the surface. Ask questions like "What brings me joy? Who am I thankful for? How have challenges led to growth?"

4. Share Gratitude
- Choose a person. Write a note detailing how a specific action or trait impacted you. Specify the situation, emotions, and your gratitude. Deliver it in person or via a thoughtful message.

5. Come to Your Senses
> Spend 5 minutes in mindfulness. Feel the warmth of sunlight on your skin, notice the vibrant colors around you, savor a favorite taste, inhale a comforting scent, and listen intently to a soothing sound.

6. Use Visual Reminders
> Place 3 visual cues strategically. Each represents a distinct gratitude. When you see them, take a moment to relive the associated moment, focusing on the details.

7. Make a Gratitude Vow
> Draft a concise vow. Specify one aspect to appreciate daily, like "family support." Place it where you can't miss it, ensuring a daily reminder and commitment.

8. Send a Gratitude Text
> Choose someone. Craft a specific message detailing a particular action, trait, or moment you appreciate. Be timely in sending it, ensuring the impact is immediate and heartfelt.

9. Perform a Random Act of Kindness
> Every day for one week, secretly place uplifting notes in public spaces. Include positive affirmations or encouraging messages to brighten someone's day.

10. Practice Three Grateful Statements
> Begin your day by vocalizing or writing 3 unique points of gratitude. Be specific and tap into emotion in order to foster deep gratitude.

Power of Symbolism and Rituals

I'm a big fan of rituals, particularly the notion of a before and after. In martial arts culture, we leave our shoes at the door, symbolizing leaving the day's troubles behind. I extend this idea to my school, where even the white floors symbolize a blank slate, akin to the concept of a white belt representing the absence of knowledge. I appreciate the power of compartmentalizing one's day, leaving work behind and preparing for the next challenge.

I find symbolism in burning a picture of a toxic person, marking a clear before and after in life. Smudging, whether tied to spirituality or not, holds significance for me. Before fights, I've smudged myself with sage to rid bad energy and create mental clarity. This ritual has proven powerful in relieving stress and anxiety.

Athletes like Simone Biles, Michael Phelps, and Michael Jordan have their routines for optimal performance. For me, it was taking showers to compartmentalize my day and signify the importance of each workout.

Rituals, like those, serve as transitions, marking a before and after, cleansing the past, and preparing for the next task.

I believe in the immense power of rituals, and it's crucial to explain them with purpose to children. This provides them with the ability to mark transitions in their lives intentionally, drawing lines between before and after, and cultivating a special mindset for whatever lies ahead.

- Leaving Shoes at the Door: Symbolizing leaving daily troubles behind.
- Listening to a Routine Song Before a Workout: Creating a mental trigger for optimal performance.
- Walking Around Home/Business, Admiring Achievements: Triggering gratitude before work or upon waking up.
- Praying or Saying Three Grateful Statements Prior to Every Meal: Cultivating mindfulness and gratitude around food.

PREPARING FOR TRIUMPH

SETTING THE STAGE FOR SUCCESS

- Nurturing Success through Habits, Routine and Environment
- Creating Artificial Challenges for Strength and Resilience

Intrinsic Motivation vs. Extrinsic Motivation: What Drives Us to Act?

When we talk about intrinsic and extrinsic motivation, we're exploring what makes us tick. Intrinsic motivation comes from inside – it's when you do something because you love it. Extrinsic motivation, on the other hand, is when outside stuff pushes you to act.

If you're intrinsically motivated, just doing the thing is enough – you enjoy it. But for those extrinsically motivated, it's about getting rewards or avoiding trouble.

And how fortunate it is to have someone intrinsically motivated, paving their way to success in the future! However, the reality is that many children lack the life experiences to make decisions independently. In such cases, I'm not hesitant to turn to extrinsic motivation to expose them to new experiences or guide them through challenging situations. Let's face it, if left to their own devices, most children might opt for ice cream for breakfast and resist trying anything new because it seems "scary." Yet, we understand that our biggest fears often arise from the unknown.

Exposing children to various aspects of life, including scholastics, physical activities, fitness, and spirituality, contributes to their growth and development, guiding them to become valuable members of society. I encourage parents to do whatever it takes, incorporating celebration and extrinsic motivation when needed, to keep their children on the right track, aligning with values that set them up for success in the future. As a reminder, if your child is already intrinsically motivated, nurture it and follow the rules to ensure that their natural gifts are not inadvertently devalued.

Researchers have delved into the effects of intrinsic and extrinsic motivations on behavior and goal pursuit. Let's break down each motivation type to understand their influence.

Getting Why We Do Stuff

Psychologists explore why we do what we do – is it because we love it inside (intrinsic) or because something outside is pushing us (extrinsic)? Sometimes, doing something just because it's fun is enough, but too many outside rewards can take away the fun.

Types of Motivation

Intrinsic motivation is doing something because it's fun for you. Extrinsic motivation is when you do stuff for a reward or to avoid getting in trouble.

Think about playing a sport because it's fun (intrinsic) or joining a contest to win a scholarship (extrinsic). Each type of motivation affects how we act.

Balancing Act: Outside vs. Inside Motivation

Research says intrinsic and extrinsic motivation affect how we behave. Extrinsic motivation helps in some cases, but giving rewards for things that are already fun can make them less fun – that's the overjustification effect.

Using rewards isn't bad, especially for not-so-fun tasks. They give feedback, make new things interesting, and help you learn new stuff.

But be careful with outside rewards. If something is already fun, too many rewards can make it feel like work, not play.

Navigating Motivation

The talk about intrinsic and extrinsic motivation isn't one-sided. Sometimes, you need outside motivation when the inside one isn't enough. It depends on the situation and what you like.

Here's what researchers found:

1. Getting rewards for easy stuff makes it less fun.
2. Good praise makes you like something even more.
3. Unexpected rewards don't spoil the fun.

Schools often use outside rewards, but if used right, they can help you feel proud and good at what you do. Things like promotions, scholarships, and bonuses can make you want to do your best.

In a nutshell, both inside and outside motivations make us do things. Knowing when to enjoy what you're doing and when outside rewards can help is the key to dealing with different situations.

Nurturing Success through Habits, Routine and Environment

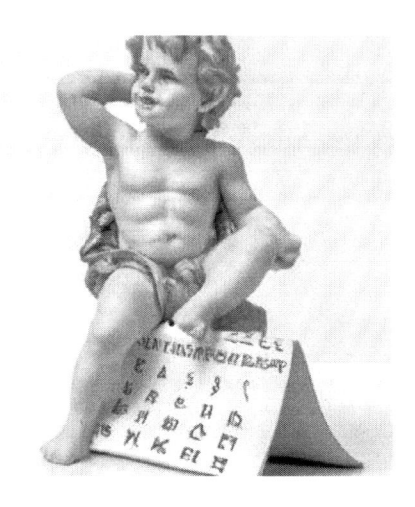

In my opinion, habits, routine, and environment hold greater importance than self-discipline. Self-discipline relies on fleeting motivation and inspiration, often guided by momentary feelings. As experienced parents, we understand that feelings can be deceptive and may not always serve our best interests. To ensure success, it's crucial to create a buffer between after-school activities, anticipating potential hiccups and fostering a stress-free environment when plans don't go as expected, such as a child having a meltdown.

The following are proven strategies for setting up success. These are versatile tips that can be adapted to any situation which requires discipline. Our goal is to make success as effortless as possible.

1. **Strategic After-School Planning**
   - ❯ How to: Plan extra time for transitions to avoid stress and overwhelm.
   - ❯ Why: Ensures a smoother flow between activities, reducing anxiety.

2. **Proactive Issue Anticipation**
   - ❯ How to: Identify potential challenges and create a supportive environment.
   - ❯ Why: Preparing for issues fosters a calm and positive atmosphere.

3. **Healthier Eating Habits Focus**
   - ❯ How to: Make nutritious foods easily accessible; limit access to junk food.
   - ❯ Why: Encourages better food choices, making healthy options the go-to.

4. **Strategic Snack Storage**
   - ❯ How to: Store snack foods in less accessible places, like a garage freezer or cupboard.
   - ❯ Why: Makes unhealthy snacks less tempting and accessible.

5. **Dedicated Homework Environment**
   - ❯ How to: Establish a specific, distraction-free space for homework.
   - ❯ Why: Enhances focus and learning by creating an optimal work environment.

Discipline is essential, but for long-term success, our primary focus should be on unwavering routines. Once a child discovers how to avoid tasks, they may consistently follow that route. Ensure an environment that makes good choices easy, and be conscious of habits, as repeated actions shape who we become. Make a conscious effort to prevent the development of detrimental habits.

"Creating Artificial Challenges for Strength and Resilience"

In my experience, these two quotes have consistently proven themselves true:

"Hard times create strong men. Strong men create good times. Good times create weak men. And weak men create hard times."

and

"Self-esteem comes from overcoming difficult things."

So, I pose this question: How can we build self-esteem in our children during good times?

Everyone faces challenges in life, but, let's be honest, progressively, most of our lives have generally become better. As parents, our goal is to provide our children with the best life possible. Sometimes, unintentionally, we remove their struggle, and statistically, we've seen the impact on each generation progressively. This leads to young adults who lack autonomy and depend on others to meet their needs and solve their challenges.

Let's reflect on the things we brag about in our lives. Whether growing up in a tough neighborhood or graduating from med school, the things that boost our self-esteem are achievements born out of overcoming struggles. Nobody brags about how easy their life was. To build true self-esteem, we've had to endure physical, mental, emotional, or social challenges. Once again, self-esteem comes from overcoming difficult things.

As a parent and mentor, my ultimate goal is to create confident, autonomous, contributing members of society who become self-sufficient, resilient human beings with next-level self-esteem.

So, what is my answer?

Create artificial challenges in good times to nurture strong children.

As a Gen Xer, one of the things that my generation often brags about is being able to walk home from school by themselves. I was doing this at the age of 6, which is completely unheard of where I live. As mentors, we can create situations that can boost a child's self esteem while still ensuring their safety. Here is how I created this scenario for my eight year old daughter.

Two blocks away from my martial arts school was my daughter's music class, and I decided a great self-esteem boosting challenge would be to have her walk from music class to the martial arts school by herself. This isn't an industrial area with high traffic and sprinkles of homeless people around.

I began prepping my daughter about a week ahead, making a big deal out of the fact that I was going to let her walk to music class by herself. During this preparation, we went over scenarios of what to do on the street, how to handle situations, and I also gave her a tactical flashlight. We worked on what to do if challenges arose. Please note that having the tactical flashlight was more of an anchor to create awareness. By putting that in her pocket, she was not thinking about what she had to do later that day, but rather about what she would do if a potential issue arose, thus rehearsing scenarios in her mind and keeping her alert.

The first time she walked to class alone, I hid around the corner, out of sight, just to observe. She earned my confidence, and I continued to encourage her to walk back by herself. Obviously, I would be aware of timelines and continue to remind her of her responsibilities. This may not seem like much, but if you are doing things that nobody else is doing, you will walk differently — with confidence and self-esteem.

Creativity and consistency are key. Life might present challenges, but are we really putting our kids in situations where they can genuinely brag about something?

"The difference between ordinary and extraordinary is the little bit extra."

Physical fitness and academics play a significant role in developing self-esteem in children.

Breaking boards in martial arts builds confidence because it is difficult. This is an artificial challenge.

School may be challenging on its own, but if you prioritize it, how can we bring our kids to the next level to set them apart from other children and make them even more confident? I personally leave this area to a professional. My son is in Kumon for reading; he is a first grader reading at a third-grade level. This has tremendously impacted his confidence, leading him to constantly brag about his reading and to copy, quote, and journal every day.

When it comes to physical fitness, I consistently run with my children. My 7-year-old son has completed his second 5K, and my daughter has participated in 10 5K runs.

In these wonderful times, autonomy, like being able to do things for themselves, is crucial. For example, if you left your kids home for a day, would they be able to take care of themselves? Could you spend a day not doing things for your children but showing them how to do things, such as cooking and laundry? What a tremendous sense of autonomy comes from that independence. Sports, fitness goals, next-level academic achievement, life experiences – all can be next-level, artificial challenges to create self-esteem in your child.

What are some artificial challenges that you can create in your life to bring your children to the next level of self-esteem in these beautiful times?

Here are some ideas that may align with your values to get your creativity flowing.

1. Physical Fitness Challenge

- Challenge: Set a physical fitness goal, such as completing a certain number of push-ups, running a specific distance, or mastering a new yoga pose.
- How to: Guide your child in creating a fitness plan. Monitor their progress, celebrate achievements, and discuss the importance of discipline and perseverance in achieving physical goals. This not only promotes a healthy lifestyle but also builds resilience and self-discipline.

2. Home Task Efficiency Challenge

- ❯ Challenge: Assign a home-related task that requires organization and efficiency, like planning and preparing a family meal or managing household chores for a week.
- ❯ How to: Support your child in planning and executing the task. Emphasize the importance of time management, attention to detail, and the satisfaction that comes from contributing to the household. This cultivates essential life skills and a sense of responsibility.

3. Public Speaking Challenge

- ❯ Challenge: Encourage your child to prepare and deliver a short speech or presentation on a topic they are passionate about.
- ❯ How to: Provide guidance on structuring the speech, practicing effective delivery, and managing stage fright. Create a supportive environment for them to showcase their speaking skills, promoting confidence and the ability to articulate thoughts in front of an audience.

Crafting Chacter through Storytelling

Now that we've explored teaching strategies and mentoring tools, let's delve into the most powerful asset in my role as a mentor: storytelling. Storytelling not only creates impactful imagery but also evokes a profound experience through the power of words. Here's my collection of moral-based classic and modern fables, proven to make a significant impact throughout history.

ANGER, REACTION AND STUBBORNNESS

- The Fence – Anger
- Catch Monkey-Stubbornness
- Potato, Egg, Coffee Bean-Reaction
- The Cockroach Theory-Reaction
- The Pencil Maker-Change Is Possible

The Fence: Anger

There once was a little boy who had a bad temper. His father gave him a bag of nails and told him that every time he lost his temper, he must hammer a nail into the fence out back.

The first day the boy had driven six nails into the fence. Over the next few weeks, as he learned to control his anger, the number of nails hammered daily gradually dwindled. He discovered it was easier to hold his temper than to drive those nails into the fence.

Finally the day came when the boy didn't lose his temper at all. He told his father about it and the father suggested that the boy now pull out one nail for each day that he was able to hold his temper.

The days passed and the young boy was finally able to tell his father that he had pulled all of the nails from the fence.

The father took his son by the hand and led him to the fence. He said, "You have done well, my son, but look at the holes in the fence. The fence will never be the same. When you say things in anger, they leave a scar just like this one. You can put a knife in a man and draw it out. It won't matter how many times you say I'm sorry, the wound is still there. A verbal wound is as bad as a physical one."

The Moral:

Control your anger toward other people. While you may not see the damage that it does, it can leave irreparable wounds that can eventually break them.

Be kind to others and think before you let your emotions get the best of you.

How to Hunt a Monkey: Stubbornness

"Do you know how hunters of old used to trap monkeys?" A man asked his child.

"Rather than chasing them up a tree or shooting arrows from below, they'd put a heavy glass jar with a narrow neck on the floor, which had the monkeys' favourite food inside.

They'd then step back and hide, waiting for the unsuspecting animal to approach.

When it did, the monkey would reach inside, clench a fist around the food, and try to pull it out. However, the narrow neck of the jar would stop the poor monkey from getting its hand out!

It'd pull and pull, but to no avail. There was simply no way to get its hand out of the jar without releasing the food.

Rather than letting go, though, the monkey would persevere, refusing to drop its dinner.

The hunters would then approach and catch it to enjoy a meal of their own."

"Don't be like that monkey," warned the man, "In life, to fight another day and grow as person, you must know when to quit, when to move on, and when to let go of whatever's holding you back."

The Moral:

Sometimes you have to let go and give up what you have now in order to receive something better in the future. Don't let stubbornness be your downfall!

The Cockroach Theory

At a restaurant, a cockroach suddenly flew from somewhere and landed on a lady. She started screaming out of fear. With a face stricken with panic and a trembling voice, she began to jump and wave both her hands in a desperate attempt to rid herself of the cockroach. Her reaction spread like wildfire, causing everyone in her group to also become panicky.

After a valiant effort, the lady succeeded in pushing the cockroach away, but to everyone's dismay, it landed on another lady in the group. Now, it was the turn of the second lady in the group to carry on the drama.

The waiter rushed forward to their rescue. In the relay of throwing, the cockroach next fell upon the waiter. The waiter stood firm, composed himself, and observed the behavior of the cockroach on his shirt. When he was confident enough, he grabbed it with his fingers and threw it out of the restaurant.

Was the cockroach responsible for their histrionic behavior? If so, then why was the waiter not disturbed? He handled it near to perfection, without any chaos.

It is not the cockroach but the inability of those people to handle the disturbance caused by the cockroach that disturbed the ladies.

It is not the shouting of your spouse, boss, parents, or kids that disturbs you, but your inability to handle the disturbances caused by their shouting.

It's not the traffic jams on the road that disturb you, but your inability to handle the disturbance caused by the traffic jam.

More than the problem itself, it's the reaction to the problem that creates chaos in life.

The women reacted, whereas the waiter responded. Reactions are always instinctive whereas responses are always thoughtful.

The Moral

True happiness doesn't come from everything in life being perfect, but from how your attitude is toward life's imperfections.

Do you react or respond?

Potato, Egg, Coffee Bean: Reaction

Once there was a girl who was complaining to her dad that her life was so hard and that she didn't know how she would get through all of her struggles. She was tired, and she felt like as soon as one problem was solved, another would arise.

Being a chef, the girl's father took her into his kitchen. He boiled three pots of water that were equal in size. He placed potatoes in one pot, eggs in another, and ground coffee beans in the final pot.

He let the pots sit and boil for a while, not saying anything to his daughter.

He turned the burners off after twenty minutes and removed the potatoes from the pot and put them in a bowl. He did the same with the boiled eggs. He then used a ladle to scoop out the boiled coffee and poured it in a mug. He asked his daughter, "What do you see?"

She responded, "Potatoes, eggs, and coffee."

Her father told her to take a closer look and touch the potatoes. After doing so, she noticed they were soft. Her father then told her to break open an egg. She acknowledged the hard-boiled egg. Finally, he told her to take a sip of the coffee. It was rich and delicious.

After asking her father what all of this meant, he explained that each of the three food items had just undergone the exact same hardship–twenty minutes inside of boiling water.

However, each item had a different reaction.

The potato went into the water as a strong, hard item, but after being boiled, it turned soft and weak.

The egg was fragile when it entered the water, with a thin outer shell protecting a liquid interior. However, after it was left to boil, the inside of the egg became firm and strong.

Finally, the ground coffee beans were different. Upon being exposed to boiling water, they changed the water to create something new altogether.

He then asked his daughter, "Which are you? When you face adversity, do you respond by becoming soft and weak? Do you build strength? Or do you change the situation?"

The Moral:

Problems are a part of life. How we react to them makes us a better individual.

The Pencil: Be the Best You Can Be

The Pencil Maker took the pencil aside, just before putting him into the box.

"There are 5 things you need to know," he told the pencil, "Before I send you out into the world. Always remember them and never forget, and you will become the best pencil you can be."

One: "You will be able to do many great things, but only if you allow yourself to be held in someone's hand."

Two: "You will experience a painful sharpening from time to time, but you'll need it to become a better pencil."

Three: "You will be able to correct any mistakes you might make."

Four: "The most important part of you will always be what's inside."

And Five: "On every surface you are used on, you must leave your mark. No matter what the condition, you must continue to write."

The pencil understood and promised to remember, and went into the box with purpose in its heart.

The takeaway? Become the best person you can be.

One: You will be able to do many great things in life if you use your gifts, and help others by giving them your gifts.

Two: You will experience a painful things from time to time, but by going through your problems in life (and not avoiding them), you will become a stronger person.

Three: You will be able to correct any mistakes you might make. Always.

Four: The most important part of you will always be what's on the inside.

And Five: Everywhere you go you will leave your mark. Do your best, do what's best. Be your best.

Only you can fulfill the purpose to which you were born to accomplish.

Never allow yourself to get discouraged and think that your life or any other is insignificant. Make changes whenever you feel it necessary. You can always make changes!

TRUST LIES BOASTING

- Scorpion and the Frog - Trust and Nature
- The Boy Who Cried Wolf - Never Lie
- Bull Crap - Self-Deception
- Four Students - Lies
- Monkey And Dolphin – Bragging

The Scorpion and the Frog : Trust and Nature

One day, a scorpion stood at the edge of a river, wanting to cross to the other side. However, scorpions can't swim, and he knew he'd never make it across on his own. As he contemplated his predicament, a frog came by.

The scorpion approached the frog and said, "Dear Frog, would you be so kind as to carry me across the river on your back? I promise I won't harm you. After all, if I sting you, we'd both drown."

The frog was naturally hesitant. "How can I trust you not to sting me?" he asked.

The scorpion replied, "Dear Frog, it would be foolish for me to sting you because if I did, we'd both perish. You must trust that I won't harm you."

The frog, seeing the logic in the scorpion's words, agreed to carry him across the river. He allowed the scorpion to climb onto his back, and they set off.

Halfway across the river, the scorpion suddenly stung the frog. The frog, in great pain and with his strength waning, asked the scorpion, "Why did you sting me? Now we'll both die."

The scorpion, as they both began to sink, replied, "I'm sorry, dear frog, but it's in my nature. I couldn't help it."

The Moral:

The fable of "The Scorpion and the Frog" teaches us that sometimes, people or creatures can't go against their inherent nature, even if it leads to their own destruction. It serves as a reminder to be cautious and use wisdom when placing trust in situations that involve going against someone's fundamental character or nature.

The Boy Who Cried Wolf: Never Lie

Once upon a time, there lived a shepherd boy who was bored watching his flock of sheep on the hill. To amuse himself, he shouted, "Wolf! Wolf! The sheep are being chased by the wolf!" The villagers came running to help the boy and save the sheep. They found nothing and the boy just laughed looking at their angry faces.

"Don't cry 'wolf' when there's no wolf boy!", they said angrily and left. The boy just laughed at them.

After a while, he got bored and cried 'wolf!' again, fooling the villagers a second time. The angry villagers warned the boy a second time and left. The boy continued watching the flock. After a while, he saw a real wolf and cried loudly, "Wolf! Please help! The wolf is chasing the sheep. Help!"

But this time, no one turned up to help. By evening, when the boy didn't return home, the villagers wondered what happened to him and went up to the hill. The boy sat on the hill weeping. "Why didn't you come when I called out that there was a wolf?" he asked angrily. "The flock is scattered now", he said.

An old villager approached him and said, "People won't believe liars even when they tell the truth. We'll look for your sheep tomorrow morning. Let's go home now".

The Moral:

Lying breaks trust. Nobody trusts a liar, even when he is telling the truth.

The Pheasant And The Bull: Self-Deception

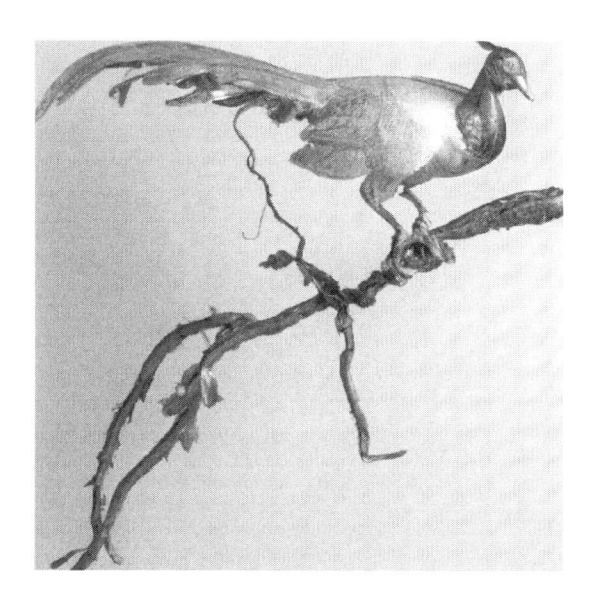

On a certain day, a bull and a pheasant were grazing on a field. The bull was grazing and the pheasant was picking ticks off the bull—a perfect partnership. Looking at the huge tree at the edge of the field, the pheasant said, "Alas, there was a time I could fly to the topmost branch of the tree. Now I do not have enough strength in my wing to even get to the first branch." The bull said nonchalantly, "Just eat a little bit of my dung every day, and watch what happens. Within two weeks, you'll get to the top." The pheasant said, "Oh come on, that's rubbish. What kind of nonsense is that?" The bull said, "Try it and see. The whole of humanity is onto it." Very hesitantly, the pheasant started pecking. And lo, on the very first day, he reached the first branch. Within a fortnight, he had reached the topmost branch. He sat there, just beginning to enjoy the scenery. The old farmer, rocking on his rocking chair, saw a fat old pheasant on top of the tree. He pulled out his shotgun and shot the bird off the tree.

The Moral:

Bull crap may get you to the top, but it never lets you stay there!

The Four Students: Lies and truth

Four friends who hated studying partied all night before their exams. They asked the Dean to give them a second chance by lying about their whereabouts. They told the Dean they had gone to a wedding the night before, and on their way back, they had a flat tire, requiring them to push the car all the way back. The Dean agreed to let them take the test again. They studied hard for the exam. On the exam day, they were made to sit in separate classrooms and were given only two questions:

- Your name
- Which tire of the car burst: a) Front Left b) Front right c) Rear left d) Rear right

The Moral:

You can run with a lie but you can't hide from the truth. It will catch you! You may be smart, but there are smarter people than you.

Monkey and the Dolphin: Bragging

A long time ago, some sailors launched their ships into the water. They used to take long journeys. For a particular long trip, one of the sailors brought his pet monkey. While they were at sea, a strong storm caused the ship to sink into the ocean.

The crew members, including the monkey and the sailors, had to swim for their lives. Their ship flipped over in the violent storm. The monkey was certain that he would drown when everyone else fell into the water. They were all in grave trouble. The monkey made an effort to protect himself. A dolphin witness the monkey battling the waters and emerged out of the sea to grab him.

They arrived at the island quickly where the monkey descended down from the dolphin's back. "Do you know this place?" the dolphin inquired of the monkey. The monkey responded, "I do, indeed! The island's king is my closest friend."

"Do you realize that I am a royal in reality?" said the monkey. Knowing that no one lived on the island, the dolphin said, "Well! Well! You are a Prince, then! You can now reign as King!". "How can I be the King?" the monkey inquired. The dolphin replied, "That is easy as you are the only species on this island so that you will be the King,". The dolphin began to swim away, and after becoming furious at this deception, it left the monkey on the island.

The Moral

The moral of the story is that those who brag unnecessarily may get into trouble. As seen in this story, the monkey was left alone on the island by a dolphin because he was just bragging about being the king's friend on this island.

Summary

Bragging and lying about things that can get you in trouble were perfectly depicted in the given story, 'Monkey and the Dolphin'. Excessive fakeness and arrogance may lead to downfall. Unnecessary bragging may only lead one to trouble and problems.

THE JOURNEY AND BEING PRESENT

> Special Olympians: More Than Winning
> Blind Race
> Being and Breathing

Special Olympians: More Than Winning

At the Seattle Special Olympics, nine contestants, all physically or mentally disabled, assembled at the starting line for the 100-yard dash. At the gun they all started out, not exactly in a dash but with a relish to run the race to the finish and win.

All, that is, except one little boy who stumbled on the asphalt, tumbled over a couple of times, and began to cry. The other eight heard the boy cry. They slowed down and looked back. Then they all turned around and went back, every one of them. One girl with Down's Syndrome bent down and kissed him and said, "This will make it better." Then all nine linked arms and walked together to the finish line. Everyone in the stadium stood, the cheering went on for several minutes.

The Morals:

People who were there are still telling the story. Why? Because deep down we know this one thing: What matters in this life is more than winning for ourselves.

What matters in this life is helping others win, even if it means slowing down and changing our course.

The Special Olympics oath is, "Let me win. But if I cannot win, let me be brave in the attempt."

Life is a Race Motivational Short Story: Enjoying the Journey

This story revolves around a young, athletic boy who was hungry for success and measured his success only by winning.

He participated in a running competition and won two races, feeling proud and important.

He then pleaded for another race and was presented with two new challengers, an elderly frail old lady and a blind man.

As the race began, the boy noticed that the elderly lady and the blind man were struggling to run. Instead of rushing ahead, he slowed down and ran alongside them, encouraging them to keep going.

Together, they reached the finish line and the boy realized that the true victory was in helping others and enjoying the journey, rather than just winning.

*The story is often used as a metaphor for the importance of slowing down, helping others, and savoring life's moments.

It emphasizes that life is not just about winning races or achieving goals, but about enjoying the journey and being kind to others.

The Moral:

Appreciate the journey, help others along the way, and find joy in the process.

Being and Breathing: Just Being

One evening, after tucking her child into bed and sharing stories of the day, a mother leaned over and whispered into their ear, "I love you."

The child smiled – and the mother smiled back – and she said, "When I'm old and reminiscing about my life, I'll cherish this moment."

A few minutes later, the child drifted off to sleep.

The mother was left with the quiet of the room and the gentle sound of her child's breathing.

She stayed awake, reflecting on all the adventures they had shared, from their first steps to their cozy bedtime routines, and all the milestones in between. These were the moments they had woven together, leading to this peaceful moment of togetherness.

At that moment, the mother realized that it didn't matter where they had been or where they were going. What mattered was the simple joy of being together.

Just being present. Breathing in sync. And resting in each other's love.

The Moral:

Life's precious moments shouldn't be overshadowed by schedules, obligations, or outside pressures. Every moment shared with loved ones is a treasure, no matter how small.

Being fully present in these moments is what gives life its true richness and meaning.

THE POWER OF WORDS AND INTENTIONS

- The Rice Experiment - Power of Intentions
- The Dog's Reflections - Power of Intentions
- Toothpaste - Think Before You Speak
- Mark Twain - Think Before You Speak

The Rice Experiment: The Power of Intentions

Dr. Masaru Emoto, a Japanese researcher best known for his experiments on the impact of positive and negative thinking on the molecular structure of water, conducted several experiments with similar outcomes. He gained widespread recognition for the rice experiment, a famous demonstration highlighting the influence of positive and negative thinking. In this experiment, Dr. Emoto placed portions of cooked rice into two containers, labeling one with "thank you" and the other with "you fool." He instructed school children to vocalize these labels daily as they passed by. After 30 days, the rice in the positively labeled container showed minimal changes, while the other container Exhibited mold and rot. Since then, this experiment has been recreated over and over again with similar results. Now, given that humans are composed of at least 60% water, would you say that this discovery holds significant implications on the power of our words? It raises the question of whether anyone can truly afford to harbor negative thoughts or intentions.

The Moral:

The moral of the story is that positive thoughts and intentions, as well as negative ones, have a tangible impact on the world around us.

The Dog's Reflections:
The Power of Intentions

Once a dog ran into a museum filled with mirrors. The museum was unique; the walls, the ceiling, the doors and even the floors were made of mirrors. Seeing his reflections, the dog froze in surprise in the middle of the hall. He could see a whole pack of dogs surrounding him from all sides, from above and below.

The dog bared his teeth and barked all the reflections responded to it in the same way. Frightened, the dog barked frantically; the dog's reflections imitated the dog and increased it many times. The dog barked even harder, but the echo was magnified. The dog, tossed from one side to another while his reflections also tossed around snapping their teeth.

The following day, the museum security guards found the miserable, lifeless dog, surrounded by thousands of reflections of the lifeless dog. There was nobody to harm the dog. The dog died by fighting with his own reflections.

The Moral:

The world doesn't bring good or evil on its own. Everything that is happening around us reflects our thoughts, feelings, wishes and actions. The world is a big mirror. So let's strike a good pose!

Mark Twain: Think Before You Speak

During a dinner, Mark Twain engaged in conversation with a lady beside him. As a gesture of courtesy, he complimented her, saying, "You are so beautiful!" Unfortunately, the lady responded with arrogance, saying, "I'm sorry, but I can't say the same for you." Unfazed, Mark Twain humorously responded, "That's alright; you could be like me, just tell a lie." The lady, feeling embarrassed, looked down.

The Morals:
1. Choose Kindness: Mark Twain's initial compliment exemplified kindness, while the lady's response lacked it. Choosing to be kind in our words can significantly impact our interactions.

2. Think Before You Speak: Mark Twain's witty response underscores the importance of thoughtful communication. Speaking without consideration may lead to embarrassment or discomfort for oneself.

3. If You Can't Say Anything Nice, Don't Say Anything at All: The story suggests that refraining from unkind remarks, especially when there's nothing positive to contribute, is a valuable practice. Choosing silence over negativity can prevent unnecessary discomfort and promote a more positive environment.

Toothpaste: Think Before You Speak

One night in July at an all-girls summer camp, the campers were gathered around in a circle for their nighttime devotions.

The counselor asked if any of the girls wanted to share something that had happened that day that impacted them.

One camper raised her hand and said a girl from another camp cabin had said something that hurt her feelings and she was really upset about it.

The camp counselor went to the bathroom to grab a tube of toothpaste.

She took the tube and squeezed it just a bit so some toothpaste came out. She then tried to put the toothpaste back in the tube, but it just created a mess. Then she squeezed the tube even more, pushing more toothpaste out and creating even more of a mess, but none of it would go back into the tube.

The counselor then told the campers, "this toothpaste represents the words you speak. Once you say something that you want to take back, it's impossible and it only creates a mess. Think before you speak, and make sure your words are going to good use before you let them out."

The Moral:

Speaking is a fundamental social skill required for living a successful life.

However, many are careless with their words, not recognizing how powerful they can be. They can have a direct impact on the outcome of a situation, creating a helpful or hurtful reaction in our world. The problem is, once words come out of your mouth, no amount of "I'm sorrys" will make them go back in. Blurting something out and then attempting to take it back is like shutting the gate after the horse has taken off.

Thinking before you speak allows you the time to consider the potential impact of your words.

Be careful when choosing where and when you let your words out. You can easily hurt other people, and once you do, you can't take it back.

THINKING OF OTHERS AND TEAMWORK

› Rabbit And The Fish - Thinking of Others
› Find Happiness - Thinking of Others/Team Work
› Strength In Unity - Team Work

Rabbit and the Fish: Thinking of Others

One day, a little rabbit went fishing, and caught nothing. The next day, he did the same thing, and also caught nothing. When he went on the third day, a big fish jumped out of the lake and shouted, "If you use carrots as fish bait again . I will kill you!"

The Moral

If you use what you think is good for others, and not what others want, you are only living in your own worthless world.

Find Happiness - Thinking of Others/Team Work

In a seminar, 50 people were given a unique task. Each person received a balloon and wrote their name on it. The balloons were then mixed up in another room. The attendees were asked to find their own balloon in 5 minutes, causing chaos as everyone searched frantically, colliding and pushing in the process.

Unable to find their own balloons, they were then instructed to pick a balloon at random and give it to the person whose name was on it. Miraculously, within minutes, everyone had their own balloon back.

The speaker explained, "This reflects our lives. We often search for happiness without knowing where to find it. True happiness is found in making others happy. By giving happiness to others, you find your own. This is the purpose of human life—the pursuit of happiness."

The Morals:
1. Think of Others: True happiness comes from considering the happiness of others.
2. The Importance of Teamwork: Collaborating and helping each other leads to success and fulfillment.

Strength In Unity: Team Work

Once upon a time, there was a man who lived in a village with his three sons. Although his three sons were hard workers, they quarreled all the time. The old man tried to unite them but failed.

Months passed by, and the man became sick. He asked his grown sons to remain united, but they failed to listen to him. At that moment, the man decided to teach them a lesson — to forget their differences and come together in unity.

The man summoned his sons. When they had gathered, he said, "I will provide you with a bundle of sticks. Separate each stick, and then break each into two. The one who finishes first will be rewarded more than the others."

And so, the sons agreed. The man provided them with a bundle of ten sticks each and then asked the sons to break each stick into pieces. The sons broke the sticks within minutes, then proceeded to quarrel among themselves again.

The old man said, "My dear sons, the game is not yet over. I will now give you another bundle of sticks. Only this time, you will have to break them together as a bundle, not separately."

The sons readily agreed and then tried to break the bundle. Despite trying their best, they could not break the sticks. The sons told their father of their failure.

The old man said, "My dear sons, see! Breaking every single stick individually was easy for you, but breaking them in a bundle, you could not do. By staying united, nobody can harm you. If you continue to quarrel, then anyone can quickly defeat you."

The old man continued, "I ask that you stay united." The three sons then understood that there's power in unity and promised their father they would all stay together.

The Moral

There's strength in unity.

KINDNESS

- The Lion And The Mouse: Kindness
- Saving Sand Dollars: Kindness/Proactivity
- Scrubbing Turtles: Kindness/Proactivity
- Androcles And The Lion: Kindness
- Angry Dog: Compassion

The Lion and The Mouse: Kindness

A Lion lay asleep in the forest, his great head resting on his paws. A timid little Mouse came upon him unexpectedly, and in her fright and haste to get away, ran across the Lion's nose. Roused from his nap, the Lion laid his huge paw angrily on the tiny creature to kill her.

"Spare me!" begged the poor Mouse. "Please let me go and some day I will surely repay you."

The Lion was much amused to think that a Mouse could ever help him. But he was generous and finally let the Mouse go.

Some days later, while stalking his prey in the forest, the Lion was caught in the toils of a hunter's net. Unable to free himself, he filled the forest with his angry roaring. The Mouse knew the voice and quickly found the

Lion struggling in the net. Running to one of the great ropes that bound him, she gnawed it until it parted, and soon the Lion was free.

"You laughed when I said I would repay you," said the Mouse. "Now you see that even a Mouse can help a Lion."

The Moral:

Kindness is never wasted.

Saving Sand Dollars: Kindness and Proactivity

A young boy and his grandfather walking down the beach. A big storm had come in the day before and there were hundreds and hundreds of sand-dollars washed up and starting to die in the sun. As they walked, the grandfather would stop from time to time, reach down, pick up a sand dollar and throw it into the ocean. Finally, the little boy asked, "Grandfather, why are you throwing them back in?" and his grandfather replied, "So that they will live." The little boy thought for a minute and said, "But grandfather, there are so many of them! What possible difference can it make?" And the grandfather, reaching down and tossing another one back into the ocean, said, "To that one, it will make all of the difference in the world."

The Moral:
The actions of one person can make a world of difference to someone else. When you see someone in need, you may never know how much of a difference your help can make in their life.

Scrubbing Turtles: Kindness and Proactivity

Every Sunday morning I take a light jog around a park near my home. There's a lake located in one corner of the park. Each time I jog by this lake, I see the same elderly woman sitting at the water's edge with a small metal cage sitting beside her.

This past Sunday my curiosity got the best of me, so I stopped jogging and walked over to her. As I got closer, I realized that the metal cage was in fact a small trap. There were three turtles, unharmed, slowly walking around the base of the trap. She had a fourth turtle in her lap that she was carefully scrubbing with a spongy brush.

"Hello," I said. "I see you here every Sunday morning. If you don't mind my nosiness, I'd love to know what you're doing with these turtles."

She smiled. "I'm cleaning off their shells," she replied. "Anything on a turtle's shell, like algae or scum, reduces the turtle's ability to absorb heat and impedes its ability to swim. It can also corrode and weaken the shell over time."

"Wow! That's really nice of you!" I exclaimed.

She went on: "I spend a couple of hours each Sunday morning, relaxing by this lake and helping these little guys out. It's my own strange way of making a difference."

"But don't most freshwater turtles live their whole lives with algae and scum hanging from their shells?" I asked.

"Yep, sadly, they do," she replied.

I scratched my head. "Well then, don't you think your time could be better spent? I mean, I think your efforts are kind and all, but there are fresh water turtles living in lakes all around the world. And 99% of these turtles don't have kind people like you to help them clean off their shells. So, no offense... but how exactly are your localized efforts here truly making a difference?"

The woman giggled aloud. She then looked down at the turtle in her lap, scrubbed off the last piece of algae from its shell, and said, "Sweetie, if this little guy could talk, he'd tell you I just made all the difference in the world."

The Moral:

You can change the world– maybe not all at once, but one person, one animal, and one good deed at a time. Wake up every morning and pretend like what you do makes a difference. It does.

Androcles and the Lion: Kindness

There was once a slave whose master was cruel to him. One day, he couldn't stand it anymore, so he fled into the forest.

On his way, he encountered a lion that was unable to walk because of a thorn in its paw. Even though he was scared, the slave mustered his courage and pulled out the thorn in the lion's paw.

When the lion was free from the thorn, he ran into the forest without hurting the slave. Soon after, the slave was caught by his master in the forest. The slave was then thrown into the lion's den by his master.

As soon as he saw the lion, the slave recognized it as the same lion he had rescued previously. As a result, the slave escaped unharmed.

The Moral:
Your good deeds will always come back to you. Do good deeds and be kind to others, and the universe will reward you

Angry Dog: Compassion

In a quaint forest, imagine stumbling upon a small dog near a tree. As you draw near, it attacks, revealing teeth and instilling fear. Yet, a closer look reveals its leg ensnared in a trap. Instantly, anger transforms into concern, recognizing the aggression stems from vulnerability and pain.

This scenario mirrors our lives—our hurtful actions often arise from our own entanglements. Through the lens of wisdom, we can cultivate compassion.

The Moral:
Anger always comes from pain. Be mindful and do your best to lead with compassion.

"Hurt people hurt people. If you don't heal from what hurt you, you'll bleed on people who never cut you."

POSITIVE OUTLOOK AND HAPPINESS

- $100 - Self Love
- Cracked Pot - Self Love
- Two Shoe Salesman - Optimism
- Put Down Negativity - Happiness
- Attitude Is Everything - Optimism
- Two Tigers - Comparison
- Dog With Job - Purpose And Nature

$100: Self-Love

A wise man began a powerful speech by holding up a $100 bill. A crowd of 200 had gathered to hear him speak. He asked, "Who would like this $100 bill?" All 200 hands went up.

He said, "I am going to give this $100 to one of you, but first, let me do this." He crumpled the bill up. Then he asked, "Who still wants it?" All 200 hands were still raised.

"Well," he replied, "What if I do this?" Then he dropped the bill on the ground and stomped on it with his shoes. He picked it up and showed it to the crowd. The bill was all crumpled and dirty. "Now who still wants it?" All the hands were still raised.

"My friends, I have just shown you a very important lesson. No matter what I did to the money, you still wanted it because it did not decrease in value. It was still worth $100. Many times in our lives, life crumples us and grinds us into the dirt. We make bad decisions or deal with poor circumstances, but no matter what has happened or what will happen, you will never lose your value.

The Moral:

Remember - dirty or clean, crumpled or finely creased, you are still very valuable!

The Cracked Pot: Self-Love

A water bearer in India had two large pots, each hung on an end of a pole that he carried across his neck. One of the pots had a crack in it, and while the other pot was perfect and always delivered a full portion of water at the end of the long walk from the stream to the master's house, the cracked pot arrived only half full. For a full two years this went on daily, with the bearer delivering only one and a half pots full of water to his masters house.

Of course, the perfect pot was proud of its accomplishments, perfect to the end for which it was made. But the poor cracked pot was ashamed of its own imperfection, and miserable that it was able to accomplish only half of what it had been made to do.

After two years of what it perceived to be a bitter failure, it spoke to the water bearer one day by the stream. "I am ashamed of myself, and I want to apologize to you."

"Why?" asked the bearer. "What are you ashamed of?'

"I have been able, for these past two years, to deliver only half my load because this crack in my side causes water to leak out all the way back to your masters house. Because of my flaws, you have to do all of this work, and you don't get full value from your efforts." The pot said.

The water bearer felt sorry for the old cracked pot, and in his compassion he said, "As we return to the master's house, I want you to notice the beautiful flowers along the path."

Indeed, as they went up the hill, the old cracked pot took notice of the sun warming the beautiful wildflowers on the side of the path, and this cheered it some. But at the end of the trail, it still felt bad because it had leaked out half its load, and so again the pot apologized to the bearer for its failure.

The bearer said to the pot, "Did you notice that there were flowers only on your side of the path, but not on the other pot's side? That's because I have always known about your flaw, and I took advantage of it. I planted flower seeds on your side of the path, and every day while we walk back from the stream, you've watered them. For two years I have been able to pick these beautiful flowers to decorate my master's table. Without you being just the way you are, he would not have this beauty to grace his house."

The Moral:

We are all cracked pots. Don't be ashamed of your flaws.
Acknowledge them, utilize them, and you too can be the cause of great beauty.

The Two Shoe Salesman: Optimism

The Two Shoe Salesman story is a well-known parable that illustrates the power of perspective and attitude.

The story goes that two shoe salesmen were sent by a shoe company to a foreign country to assess the market for their product.

The first salesman arrived and immediately sent a message back to the company saying, "There is no potential here – nobody wears shoes."

The second salesman arrived and sent a message back saying, "This is a fantastic opportunity – nobody wears shoes!"

The story demonstrates how two people can look at the same situation and interpret it completely differently based on their mindset and attitude.

The second salesman had a positive outlook and saw the potential in the situation, while the first salesman had a negative outlook and saw only the obstacles.

The Moral:

There is great power in a growth mindset. Maintain a positive attitude in order to succeed in any situation.

Put Down the Negativity: Happiness

In a classroom full of college students, a professor poured water into a glass. I expected him to ask the typical "glass half empty or half full" question. Instead, the professor asked, "How heavy is this glass of water?" Students shouted out answers ranging from eight ounces to sixteen ounces.

He replied, "The absolute weight of this glass doesn't matter. It all depends on how long I hold it. If I hold it for a minute or two, it's fairly light. If I hold it for an hour straight, it's weight might make my arm ache a little. If I hold it for a day straight, my arm will likely cramp up and feel completely numb and paralyzed, forcing me to drop the glass to the floor. In each case, the weight of the glass doesn't change, but the longer I hold it, the heavier it feels to me."

As the class shook their heads in agreement, he continued, "Your stresses and worries in life are very much like this glass of water. Think about them for a while and nothing happens. Think about them a bit longer and you begin to ache a little. Think about them all day long, and you will feel completely numb and paralyzed — incapable of doing anything else until you drop them."

The Moral:

It's important to remember to let go of your stresses and worries. No matter what happens during the day, as early in the evening as you can, put all your burdens down. Don't carry them through the night and into the next day with you. If you still feel the weight of yesterday's stress, it's a strong sign that it's time to put the glass down.

Attitude is Everything: Optimism

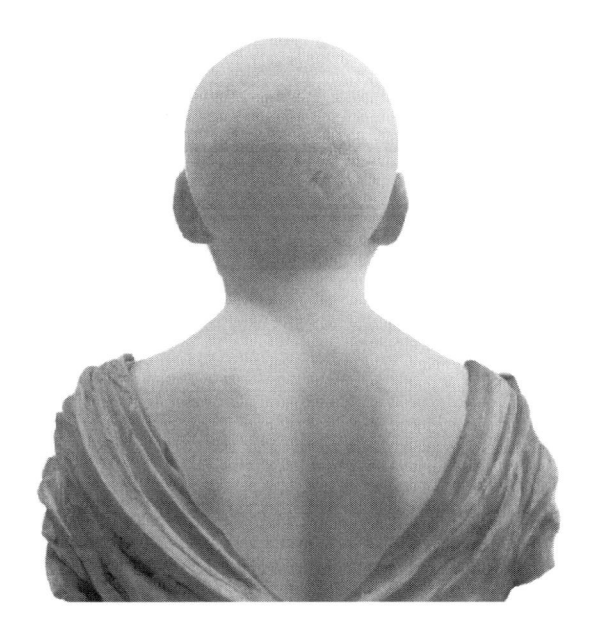

There once was a woman who woke up one morning, looked in the mirror, and noticed she had only three hairs on her head.

"Well." she said. "I think I'll braid my hair today." So she did, and she had a wonderful day.

The next day she woke up, looked in the mirror and saw that she had only two hairs on her head.

"Hmmm." she said, "I think I'll part my hair down the middle today." So she did, and she had a grand day.

The next day she woke up, looked in the mirror and noticed that she had only one hair on her head.

"Well," she said, "today I'm going to wear my hair in a pony tail." So she did and she had a fun, fun day.

The next day she woke up, looked in the mirror and noticed that there wasn't a single hair on her head.

"YEAH!" she exclaimed, 'I don't have to fix my hair today!"

Attitude is everything!

The Moral:

"The human being is born with an incurable capacity for making the best of things"

~ Helen Keller

Two Tigers: Comparison

Two tigers – one was in a cage, and the other in the wilderness. Both thought that that its own plight was bad, and each admire the other's situation and finally decided to swop positions. Not long after, both tigers died, one of hunger, and another died of loneliness.

The Moral:

We often feel dissatisfied with our own circumstances and envy others, yet in reality, others may be envious of our situation.

"Comparison is the thief of joy," -Teddy Roosevelt

A Dog Without a Job: Nature, Purpose and Happiness

Once, there lived a dog, an Australian Shepherd. This shepherd was born to herd sheep but unlike other herding dogs, it spent it's days inside. Deep down, the dog longed to be a herder, but attempting to herd furniture inside the house only led to chaos. Eventually, it acted out regularly because its needs were not being met, he became uncomfortable, testy, and tore the house apart. Thankfully, the family recognized that it was not the dog's fault; it was just its nature. They decided to make some adjustments in its life to fulfill its needs and follow its instincts.

They created a make-believe pasture in the yard and introduced sheep. The dog's joy knew no bounds! Instead of causing havoc indoors, it found purpose in caring for the sheep. The dog transformed from a troublesome indoor companion into a dedicated shepherd, illustrating the profound impact of staying true to oneself.

Human nature is to run, hunt, gather, and create. Much like the dog, if we do not continue to stay active, it will affect us negatively.

The Morals:
1. "A happy dog has a job."
2. "Keep busy; idle time invites trouble."
3. "Human nature thrives in running, hunting, gathering, and creating." Like the dog suffered when inactive, staying engaged brings a positive impact to our lives

POWER OF BELIEF

- Elephant On Rope: Limiting Beliefs
- Jumping Frogs: The Effect of Beliefs
- Swimming Experiment: Power of Belief
- Roger Bannister: Breaking Limiting Beliefs

The Elephant Rope: Limiting Beliefs

Behind the scene at a local circus, a very privileged man was passing by the elephants, he suddenly stopped, confused by the fact that these huge creatures were being held by only a small rope tied to their front leg. No chains, no cages. It was obvious that the elephants could, at anytime, break away from their bonds but for some reason, they did not.

He saw a trainer nearby and asked why these animals just stood there and made no attempt to get away. "Well," trainer said, "when they are very young and much smaller we use the same size rope to tie them and, at that age, it's enough to hold them. As they grow up, they are conditioned to believe they cannot break away. They believe the rope can still hold them, so they never try to break free."

The man was amazed. These animals could at any time break free from their bonds but because they believed they couldn't, they were stuck right where they were.

The Moral:

Like the elephants, how many of us go through life hanging onto a belief that we cannot do something, simply because we failed at it once before?

Failure is part of learning; we should never give up the struggle in life.

Jumping Frogs: The Effect of Beliefs

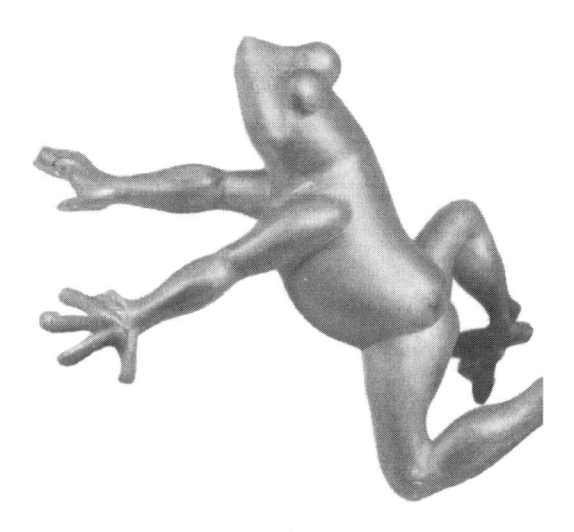

A group of frogs was hopping through the forest when two of them accidentally hopped into a deep pit. The other frogs stood around the pit, and, seeing how deep it was, they told the two frogs that they couldn't help them–there was no hope.

However, fighting for their lives, the two frogs ignored the others and started to try jumping out of the pit.

The frogs at the top continued to tell the frogs in the pit to give up, as there was no way they would be able to jump out.

After trying over and over, one of the frogs listened to the others and gave up, accepting his fate and falling to his death. But the other frog continued to jump with all of his might. The crowd of frogs yelled down the pit for the frog to just stop–he wouldn't make it.

But the frog jumped even harder and persisted until he finally got out. Upon reaching the top, the other frogs said, "We thought there was no way any frog could jump that high–couldn't you hear us?"

The frog then signaled to the others that he was deaf, and he thought that the frogs standing around the pit were encouraging him the whole time.

The Moral:

Others' words can greatly impact your attitude and actions. Ignore the naysayers. Only engage with those who will encourage and believe in your ability to succeed.

Furthermore, think about what you say to people before speaking so you can make sure what you're saying is supportive. Your support (or lack thereof) could make the difference between success and failure.

Swimming Experiment: Power of Belief

During a brutal experiment from the 1950's by Dr. Curt Richter, who tested rats' ability to swim before they gave up. Rats typically lasted about 15 minutes before drowning. In a second experiment, Richter rescued the rats right before exhaustion, allowing them to rest for a few minutes, and then put them back in the water. Surprisingly, these rats swam for nearly 60 hours more!. This experiment illustrates the power of hope. When we believe our circumstances are temporary and change is possible, we can achieve remarkable things.

The Moral:

The message is clear: Stay hopeful. Hope can be the transformative factor that changes outcomes.

Roger Bannister: Breaking Limiting Beliefs

In 1954, the idea of running a mile in under 4 minutes was deemed impossible by many, including doctors, psychologists, and runners who believed it exceeded human limits. However, Roger Bannister, a 25-year-old Oxford student and top runner, challenged this notion. Despite skepticism, he aimed to break the 4-minute barrier. In early 1954, he ran the mile in 3:59.4 and collapsed at the finish line, making everyone think he was done for. To their surprise, Roger Bannister popped back up, revealing that the limitation was a mental barrier, not a physical one.

Within a year, 37 runners shattered the belief barrier, achieving a sub-4-minute mile.

Reflection: the physical barrier preventing a sub-four-minute mile wasn't overcome by a sudden leap in human ability. Instead, it was the change in thinking that made the difference.

Bannister demonstrated that breaking the four-minute mile was possible.

The Moral:

Our beliefs and mindsets can either limit or expand our world and changing our thinking can break barriers.

LIFE HAPPENS FOR ME AND GROWTH

- Kintsugi: Tragedy
- "Helping" A Butterfly: Growth
- Lobster: Growth
- Maybe: Life Happens For Me
- Burning Hut: Life Happens For Me

Kintsugi: Tragedy

In Western culture, when a dish or pot breaks, it's often discarded. However, in Japan, there's a beautiful art practice known as Kintsugi.

Kintsugi is a Japanese art form and philosophy centered on repairing broken pottery and ceramics. The term "kintsugi," often referred to as "the art of precious scars," involves mending shattered or cracked objects with a special lacquer mixed with powdered gold, silver, or other precious metals. The result isn't just a functional repair but also a transformation of the damaged item into a unique and often more beautiful piece.

The philosophy of kintsugi emphasizes the acceptance of imperfections and the celebration of an object's history and journey. Rather than concealing or disguising the cracks, kintsugi enhances them by filling them with precious metals. This approach reflects the idea that flaws and breakages are integral to an object's story and contribute to its beauty.

Kintsugi serves not only as a technique for repairing ceramics but also as a symbol of resilience, the embrace of imperfections, and the discovery of beauty within imperfection. It has inspired various forms of art, design, and philosophical discussions regarding the value of imperfection in our lives.

The Moral:

In our lives, tragedy is inevitable, and as we piece ourselves back together, our experiences make us even more beautiful.

"Helping" a Butterfly: Growth

One day, a girl came upon a cocoon, and she could tell that a butterfly was trying to hatch.

She waited and watched the butterfly struggle for hours to release itself from the tiny hole. All of a sudden, the butterfly stopped moving–it seemed to be stuck.

The girl then decided to help get the butterfly out. She went home to get a pair of scissors to cut open the cocoon. The butterfly was then easily able to escape, however, its body was swollen and its wings were underdeveloped.

The girl still thought she had done the butterfly a favor as she sat there waiting for its wings to grow in order to support its body. However, that wasn't happening.

The butterfly was unable to fly, and for the rest of its life, it could only move by crawling around with little wings and a large body.

Despite the girl's good intentions, she didn't understand that the restriction of the butterfly's cocoon and the struggle the butterfly had to go through in order to escape served an important purpose.

As butterflies emerge from tight cocoons, it forces fluid from their body into their wings to prepare them to be able to fly.

The Moral:
The struggles that you face in life help you grow and get stronger.

There is often a reason behind the requirement of doing hard work and being persistent. When enduring difficult times, you will develop the necessary strength that you'll need in the future.

Without having any struggles, you won't grow–which means it's very important to take on personal challenges for yourself rather than relying on other people to always help you.

The Lobster: Growth

Have you ever heard the story of the lobster? Well, it's a fascinating one. You see, a lobster is a soft, mushy animal that lives inside a rigid shell. As the lobster grows, it has to leave that shell and find a new one. But there's a period of vulnerability while the lobster is soft and exposed. During this time, the lobster is at risk, as its new shell hasn't yet hardened.

Now, here's the crucial part of the story. The stimulus for a lobster to grow is discomfort. When the lobster feels uncomfortable in its tight shell, it knows it's time to leave it behind and find a new one. So, the lobster seeks out a safe crevice, sheds its old shell, and waits for a new one to form. This process of growth through discomfort repeats throughout the lobster's life.

The moral of the story is this: Just like lobsters, we humans often need discomfort, challenges, and adversity to grow. Our struggles and challenges are like the discomfort of the lobster's tight shell. They can lead us to shed our old beliefs, habits, and limitations, and enable us to emerge stronger and more resilient.

So, when you face difficult times, remember the lobster. Embrace the discomfort and see it as an opportunity for growth and transformation. After all, it's often through our challenges that we become the best versions of ourselves."

The Moral:

Remember that discomfort serves as the stimulus for growth, so embrace the process and recognize it as a vital element.

Maybe: Life Happens For Me

There is a story of an old farmer who had worked his crops for many years. One day his horse ran away. Upon hearing the news, his neighbors came to visit.

"Such bad luck," they said sympathetically.

"Maybe," the farmer replied. The next morning, the horse returned, bringing with it three other wild horses. "How lucky you are," the neighbors exclaimed.

"Maybe," replied the old man. The following day, his son tried to ride one of the untamed horses, was thrown, and broke his leg.

The neighbors again came and said, "You are so unfortunate."

"Maybe," answered the farmer. The day after, military officials came to the village to draft young men into the army. Seeing that the son's leg was broken, they passed him by.

Once again, the neighbors came around and said, "You are so fortunate, you are so lucky."

"Maybe," said the farmer.

The Moral:

Often, luck is what you make of it, and bad luck is simply a matter of perspective.

"Life happens for us... Not to us."

The Burning Hut: Life Happens for Me

The only survivor of a shipwreck washed up on a small, uninhabited island. Every day he scanned the horizon for help, but none seemed forthcoming. Exhausted, he eventually managed to build a little hut out of driftwood and dried palm fronds to protect him from the elements and to store his few possessions.

One day, after scavenging for food, he arrived home to find his little hut in flames, the smoke rolling up to the sky. The worst had happened; everything was lost. He was stung with grief and anger.

Early the next day, however, he was awakened by the sound of a ship that was approaching the island. It had come to rescue him. "How did you know I was here?" asked the weary man of his rescuers.

"We saw your smoke signal," they replied

It is easy to get discouraged when things are going bad. But we shouldn't lose heart, sometimes those bad things are just what we need to be rescued.

The Moral:

Remember next time your little hut is burning to the ground -- it just may be a smoke signal.

PROXIMITY

- Five Monkeys: Blind Adherence
- Raised By Chickens

Monkey Experiment: Blind Adherence

In a famous experiment, scientists put five monkeys in a room with a large bunch of bananas. There was also a ladder in the middle of the room. Every time a monkey tried to climb the ladder to retrieve the bananas, everyone, including that monkey, gets a surprise shower with cold water! Brr!

After a little while, they change one of the monkeys for a new one who doesn't know about the cold water surprise. When the new monkey tries to climb the ladder, the others stop it because they remember the cold water. Even if they don't know why, they just know it's not a good idea.

This keeps happening - they switch monkeys, and the new ones learn from the others not to climb the ladder. After a bit, none of the monkeys in the room have ever felt the cold water, but they still stop anyone from climbing the ladder because that's what everyone else is doing.

The Morals:

The lesson here is about doing things without really knowing why, just because everyone else is doing them.

Make sure you think and ask questions about why we do things and not just do them because others are doing the same.

Raised By Chickens: Proximity

Imagine two children born at the same time but instead of being raised by humans, they were raised by animals-two very different animals.

First, there's Jake. Think of him like a mini Tarzan, raised by a bunch of strong lions. They taught him how to survive, lead, and hunt like a pro. Jake became a bold kid, walking around like he's saying, "I'm the boss of this jungle!"

Now, meet Sally. She had a different upbringing—raised by a group of chickens. Yep, you heard it right, chickens. Sally clucked before she talked, pecked at her food, and scratched at life. Those chickens taught her to stay low and not be daring.

Here's a simple idea: "You become the average of the five people you spend the most time with." Jake, with his lion friends, learned courage and pride. But Sally, with her chicken pals, had a harder time feeling like a winner.

Jake confidently went through life, supported by strong friends. Sally, on the other hand, hung out with cluckers who preferred scratching around instead of facing challenges.

So, here's the big idea, my friends. Be with people who have the spirit you want. Whether it's the roar of lions, the quickness of monkeys, or the friendship of your human pals, make sure your friends are awesome. In the jungle of life, be the one roaring, not just clucking around. That's the power of your buddies!

The Morals

"Show me your friends and I will show you who you are. "

"We are the average of the five people that we spend the most time with"

"You can't soar with the Eagles"

PERSEVERANCE AND AN UNBREAKABLE SPIRIT

- Digging for Gold: Perseverance
- Bucket of Cream: Perseverance / Unbreakable Spirit
- The Donkey and the Well: Perseverance/Unbreakable Spirit
- Unbreakable Runner: Perseverance / Unbreakable Spirit

Digging For Gold: Perseverance

During the time of the Gold Rush, an ambitious man from Colorado acquired mining equipment and started digging for gold. After considerable effort, he found a small vein of gold nuggets, proving there was potential in his endeavor. Excited, he went out and secured financing to purchase more equipment, continuing his mining venture.

However, as time passed, any sight of gold disappeared. Discouraged, the man sold his equipment to a junk dealer and returned home. The junk dealer, seeking expert advice, consulted a mining engineer who determined that the gold deposit the man was seeking was just three feet away from where the previous owner had stopped.

The Moral:

When things start to get hard, try to persevere through the adversity.

Many people give up on their dreams because the work becomes too difficult, tedious, or tiresome—but often, you're closer to the finish line than you may think, and if you push just a little harder, you will succeed.

The Two Mice in the Bucket of Cream: Perseverance / Unbreakable spirit

Once upon a time, two mice fell into a large bucket of cream. This bucket of cream was so deep and slippery that there was no way for them to climb out. They swam and swam, but it seemed hopeless.

The first mouse, after a while, grew tired and despondent. He couldn't see any way out, and so he stopped swimming and said, "There's no use. I can't keep going." And with that, he drowned in the cream.

The second mouse, however, was made of sterner stuff. He wasn't about to give up. He kept paddling and paddling, determined not to be defeated by the cream. He kept thinking, "I can't give up. I have to keep going." He kicked and paddled, splashing cream everywhere.

Hours passed, and the cream seemed as thick as ever. But the mouse refused to quit. He kept churning and churning until, miraculously, the cream began to thicken and turn into butter. The mouse had churned the cream into butter with his relentless effort. Now, there was a solid mass in the bucket, and he climbed out to safety.

The Moral

Persistence and determination can turn even the most challenging situations in your favor. When faced with adversity, don't give up. Keep trying, keep working, and you might just find a way out of the toughest situations.

The Donkey Who Fell Down a Well: Perseverance/Unbreakable spirit

One day a farmer's donkey fell down into a well. For hours, the farmer tried to figure out what to do. Finally he decided the animal was old and the well needed to be covered up anyway; it just wasn't worth it to retrieve the donkey.

He invited his neighbors to come over and help him. They all grabbed a shovel and began to shovel dirt into the well. At first, the donkey realized what was happening and cried horribly.

Then, to everyone's amazement, he quieted down. A few shovel loads later, the farmer finally looked down the well and was astonished at what he saw.

With every shovel of dirt that hit his back, the donkey was doing something amazing. He would shake it off and take a step up. As the farmer's neighbors continued to shovel dirt on top of the animal, he would shake it off and step up. Pretty soon, everyone was amazed as the donkey stepped up over the well and trotted off!

The Moral:

Life is going to shovel dirt on you - all kinds of dirt. The trick to getting out of the well is to shake it off and take a step up. Each of our troubles is a stepping stone. We can get out of the deepest wells by not stopping, never giving up! Shake it off and take a step up!

The Unbreakable Runner: Perseverance/Unbreakable spirit

Imagine you're gearing up for the Great Friendship Race. You're not just any racer – you're special. Hurt your legs? No problem! You'd be the coolest hopper, jumping your way to victory with a big grin.

But wait, what if some magical mischief hits, and your other leg gets a little banged up? No sweat! You'd be the most awesome crawler, giggling and navigating the race with an unstoppable spirit.

Now, let's talk about your arms. Picture a tricky part making them tired or sore. What's your move? Roll, my friend! Imagine yourself rolling like a happy tumbleweed, bringing joy to everyone watching.

And here's the kicker – nothing can stop you! You're like a superhero with an unbreakable spirit and an indomitable will, ready to tackle any challenge with a big, brave heart.

So, go ahead, champion! Picture yourself in that race, overcoming every hurdle with a hop, a crawl, or a roll. You're unstoppable, and the adventure is all yours. Keep that magical spirit shining bright!

The Morals:

Never give up! Work around any challenges! You can always do 'something' so no excuses... Find a way!

I MUST have an unbreakable spirit!

I MUST have an indomitable will!

TAKING ACTION

- Socrates: Burning Desire
- Take the Leap Riddle: Take Action
- Rock In The Road: Take Action
- Wiseman Jokes: Take Action
- Nothing Comes From Nothing: Take Action/Proactivity
- Power Of Visualization: Take Action

Socrates and the Secret to Success: Burning Desire

Once a young man asked the wise man, Socrates, the secret to success. Socrates patiently listened to the man's question and told him to meet him near the river the next morning for the answer. The next morning Socrates asked the young man to walk with him towards the river. As they went in the river the water got up to their neck. But to the young man's surprise, Socrates ducked him into the water.

The young man struggled to get out of the water, but Socrates was strong and kept him there until the boy started turning blue. Socrates pulled the man's head out of the water. The young man gasps and took a deep breath of air. Socrates asked, 'What did you want the most when your head was in the water?" The young man replied, "Air." Socrates said, "That is the secret to success. When you want success as badly as you wanted the air while you were in the water, then you will get it. There is no other secret."

The Moral:

A burning desire is the starting point of all accomplishment. Just like a small fire cannot give much heat, a weak desire cannot produce great results.

Take the Leap Riddle: Take Action

There's an old riddle that says five frogs are sitting on a lily pad. One decides to jump off. How many are left?

If your answer is "four", thank your math teacher for your excellent skills. Unfortunately, this is not a test of your math abilities.

It's a life problem.

The correct answer is "five". Yes, all five are still sitting there on the lily pad.

The one frog only decided to jump... But hasn't.

Life is not a spectator sport. It is a contact sport. There are no practice sessions and you've been in the game since day one.

As cliche as it seems 'The journey starts with a single step' — not by thinking about taking that step.

The Moral:

Be the frog who not only decides to jump off the lily pad but actually jumps.

Rock in the Road: Take Action

Many, many years ago, there was a small village that was very distinguished. Most of the residents were very dignified and appreciated order within their small community. Gardens were manicured perfectly. Houses were clean. Walkways were swept. Everything in this small community ran smoothly.

There was only one problem. The small town only had one main road. Along this road you could find people walking, some on horseback, others in wagons, and herders moving their animals to market. The problem was, there was a large rock right in the middle of the road.

Every day, the patrons had to swerve around this rock.

Everyone who avoided the large rock blamed the emperor for not keeping the main street in the village in better repair. They'd say, "That rock is an irritation, why doesn't the emperor have his men remove it?" Or, "What a bother, the emperor needs to fix that." And, "When's the emperor going to fix that? A large rock in the road is so unbecoming of our nice village."

One day, a peasant was sitting on the side of the road, watching all of the traffic avoid this large rock. After a while, the peasant walked into the road, and began moving the rock. The people just kept passing, with no offer to help the peasant move the rock. After some time and effort, the peasant moved the rock clear of the traffic. When he went back to the original spot of the rock, he found that the rock had been covering something. Upon further investigation, he pulled a large box from the ground. It was a box full of treasure.

The peasant took his newfound box to the emperor. He told the emperor his story of moving the rock, and finding the box of treasure buried beneath it.

The emperor inquired, "You moved the rock that was in the middle of the main road?"

The peasant replied that he had.

The emperor informed the peasant that he may keep the treasure for himself. The emperor had known of the treasure for years. It was put there as a prize for the person that would take the initiative to do the right thing and move the rock.

The Moral:

Many people see problems in the road and all they do is pass those problems, complain, and then blame someone else for the problem. It is those people who see a problem and take the time to fix that problem that deserve the biggest rewards in life.

A Wise Man's Jokes: Take Action

A wise man once faced a group of people who were complaining about the same issues over and over again. One day, instead of listening to the complaints, he told them a joke and everyone cracked up laughing.

Then, the man repeated the joke. A few people smiled.

Finally, the man repeated the joke a third time–but no one reacted.

The man smiled and said, "You won't laugh at the same joke more than once. So what are you getting from continuing to complain about the same problem?"

The Moral:

You're not going to get anywhere if you keep complaining about the same problem but do nothing to fix it.

Don't waste your time complaining, expecting other people to continue to react to your complaints. Instead, take action to make a change.

Spend 5% of your time on a problem (acknowledge it)and 95% of your time on a solution

Nothing Comes from Nothing: Take Action/Proactivity

In a quiet suburban neighborhood, the mantra "nothing comes from nothing" was instilled in the hearts of a father and his daughter. They shared a unique bond, running together regularly, even when the daughter's favorite TV shows beckoned.

One ordinary day, the father approached his daughter as she lounged in front of the television. "It's time to run," he declared. However, the young girl wasn't feeling particularly motivated that day. She mumbled her reluctance. Sensing her mood, the father made a proposition. "I understand it's a rough day, but we must honor our commitments. How about we compromise? We'll do a run-walk at three-quarters of our usual distance." The girl hesitantly agreed, and together they embarked on their journey.

As they followed their usual running route, they unexpectedly crossed paths with some neighborhood friends who had created an enormous haunted house. The father, seeing the excitement in his daughter's eyes, asked, "Would you like to check this out?" With unbridled enthusiasm, she exclaimed, "Absolutely!" The father made a deal. "Let's finish the first half of our run, and then we can join in the fun."

Eagerly, the young girl sprinted like never before, eager to seize this thrilling opportunity. Inside the haunted house, she was delighted by the special effects and an abundance of candy. Her smile seemed permanent.

On their way back home, the father paused during their jog and looked into his daughter's eyes. He asked, "Are you happy that you went for a run today instead of staying on the couch?" Her response was resounding, "Absolutely. It was one of the best experiences of my life." The father then shared a valuable lesson. "Remember that feeling. Sitting on the couch doing nothing brings you nothing. But when you venture out into the world, explore, and stay active, you will always have momentum, and opportunities will come your way."

They continued their running routine, and every time an opportunity to make a difference emerged, such as rescuing a lost dog or helping a homeless man, the father and daughter seized it. Each time, the father would kneel and ask, "Aren't you glad you ventured into the world today and made a difference instead of staying on the couch?" Their shared experiences and commitment to action not only brought them closer but also allowed them to create a world of meaning beyond the confines of their living room.

The Moral:

When you're active and explore, you unlock exciting opportunities and meaningful moments. The story tells us sitting idle might not bring those awesome experiences, so it's important to get up, stay engaged, and make a positive impact on the world around you.

The Power of Visualization: Take Action-Outside the Box

There's a study conducted by Dr. Blaslotto at the University of Chicago in 1996 on visualization.

Dr. Blaslotto's study was conducted by asking a group of students who had been randomly selected to take a series of free-throws. The percentage of made free throws were tallied. The students were then divided into three groups and asked to perform three separate tasks over a 30 day period.

> » The first group was told not to touch a basketball for 30 days, no practicing or playing basketball whatsoever.

- The second group was told to practice shooting free throws for a half hour a day for 30 days
- The third group was to come to the gym every day for 30 days and spend a half hour with their eyes closed, simply visualizing hitting every free-throw.
- After the 30 days all three groups were asked to come back and take the same number of free-throws they had in the beginning of the study.
- The first group of students who did not practice at all showed no improvement
- The second group had practiced every day and showed a 24% improvement
- The third group however, the group which had simply visualized successful free-throws, showed a 23% improvement

The measurable improvement in the group that purely visualized the exercise was virtually the same as the group who had physically practiced.

The Morals:

Visualization could be just as powerful as performing the actual event.

This is a powerful tool and a great life lesson. In certain instances, we may have limitations such as location, physical ability/injury, or available finances that may momentarily halt us from performing an activity. With the power of visualization, we can get just as closer to the results we want at any time we want without any external resources needed.

CONSISTENCY, EFFORT, HARD WORK AND PREPARATION

- Carpenter's Retirement: Effort
- Two Lumberjacks- Prep: Preparation
- Tortoise And The Hare: Consistency
- The Crow And The Pitcher: Hard Work
- Soar Like An Eagle: Hard Work

Carpenter's Retirement: Effort

There was an old carpenter who was going to retire, and because his boss could not bear to let him go, he asked the old carpenter to build a house before he leaves. Although the old carpenter agreed, his heart was already not on his job – he used lousy materials, cut corners, and the house he built was the worst project he had ever been a part of. When the house was ready, and the carpenter handed the keys over to his boss, he responded by saying, 'I have a huge surprise for you.' The boss then proceeded to hand the keys back to the carpenter. The old carpenter was saddened and ashamed to learn that the house he had built was actually for himself.

The Moral:

Everything we do in life, we are actually doing for ourselves so we must make sure we do the best we can.

Two Lumberjacks: Preparation

Two lumberjacks decided to have a contest to see who could chop the most wood. One was a young, energetic man who could chop relentlessly. He was convinced he would win easily against the older lumberjack who was on the back end of his tree felling days.

The rules were simple. Whoever chopped the most wood during their shift would win. They were working on opposite side of a little ridge, so they could hear each other, but couldn't see their progress. What the younger lumberjack could see though were the numerous breaks the veteran kept taking. Over and over, they energetic fellow would see his competition sitting up by the tent, axe on his lap.

At the end of the day, both men climbed the ridge to assess who the victor was.

Much to the surprise of the younger lumberjack, the older many had a pile that dwarfed his own. He was convinced the man cheated.

"How could you have won? I saw all the breaks you were taking!"

The experienced lumberjack chuckled. "You thought those were breaks? I was sharpening my axe."

The Moral:

Those who fail to prepare are preparing to fail.

The Tortoise and the Hare: Hard Work and Consistency

A tortoise and a hare had an argument about who was faster. They decided to settle the argument with a race. They agreed on a route and started off the race.

The hare shot ahead and ran briskly for some time. Then, seeing he was far ahead of the tortoise, he thought he'd sit down and rest for a while before continuing the race. He sat down under a tree and soon fell fast asleep.

The tortoise, plodding along, soon overtook him, passed him, crossed the finish line, and won the race.

The hare woke up and realized he'd lost.

Many people will conclude that Slow and Steady win the race. When I read the story, I feel that the real lesson is not about the tortoise at all, it's about the hare.

The hare made a huge mistake, believing in its ability but then not actually proving it. In real life, you may have that great skill, one which everyone agrees, but you must still showcase that skill to win the competition.

The Moral:

Hard work and consistency will beat talent when talent does not work hard enough.

The Crow and the Pitcher: Hard Work and Consistency

Once upon a time, in a parched land where water was scarce, a thirsty crow came across a pitcher. The crow was desperate for a drink, but when it looked inside, it saw that the water was at the bottom, beyond the reach of its beak.

The crow tried and tried to reach the water but couldn't. It was about to give up when it had an idea. The clever crow began dropping pebbles one by one into the pitcher. With each pebble, the water level rose a little bit.

The crow continued to drop pebble after pebble until, at last, the water level had risen enough for the crow to take a drink and quench its thirst.

The Moral:
This fable teaches us that with ingenuity and determination, we can find solutions to even the most challenging problems. It encourages us to think creatively when faced with difficult situations.

Soar Like an Eagle: Lean into Hard Work

Did you know that an eagle can foresee when a storm is approaching long before it breaks?

Instead of hiding, the eagle will fly to some high point and wait for the winds to come.

When the storm hits, it sets its wings so that the wind can pick it up and lift it above the storm. While the storm rages below, the eagle soars above it. The eagle does not escape or hide from the storm; instead, it uses the storm to lift it higher. It rises on the stormy winds which others dread.

When the storm of life or challenges hits us, we can rise above them and soar like the eagle that rides the storm's winds. Don't be afraid of the storms or the challenges in your life. Use it to lift you higher in your life.

The Moral:

Face life's challenges like an eagle faces a storm. Don't hide or escape; instead, rise above difficulties, using them to lift yourself higher and soar beyond the storms of life.

PROCRASTINATION AND NEGLIGENCE

- Frog For Dinner: Procrastination
- Mouse In The Rice: Procrastination
- A Snowball Effect: Negligence

Frogs for Dinner: Procrastination

A lady was once heating up a pot of water on a gas stove with the intent of cooking pasta for her family for dinner.

A frog fell into the pot while it was sitting on the stove. While it wasn't his intention to be stuck in a pot of water, he didn't try to escape. He was comfortable enough as he was.

The lady soon turned on the flame to begin boiling the water.

As the water's temperature began to rise, the frog was able to adjust his body temperature accordingly, so he remained in the pot without trying to do anything to change the situation.

However, as the water approached its boiling point, the frog's body temperature could no longer keep up. He finally tried to jump out of the pot, but with water temperature continuing to increase, he didn't have it in him to make the leap. It was too late for the frog to save himself.

The Moral:

Things don't always go as planned in life, and they certainly don't always go the way we want them to. But, no matter how bad a situation is, it's critical to be proactive and face the problem head-on. Unlike the frog, who waited until the last minute to try to do anything about the problem he was clearly facing, it's important to project the future outcomes of the obstacles that hinder you and mediate them before they get past the point of no return. You must avoid wasting your time and take appropriate action before problems become too much to handle.

Mouse In the Rice: Procrastination

A mouse fell into half a tank of rice, and was delighted. After checking that there was no danger, he ate the rice and fell asleep immediately. Such is life, and he ate and slept in the tank for a while. But after a while, the rice is depleted.

It was only then that he realized that he was now too deep into the pot and the ability to climb out was no longer a possibility.

The Moral:

Not doing your homework, not working out. Not saving not taking care of yourself. You spent the whole day eating being lazy and not doing the work you're supposed to do you will eventually put yourself into a dark chasm, which is nearly impossible to get out of.

A Snowball Effect: Negligence

Years ago, I had the privilege of teaching a remarkable young student with ADHD. His faithful companion was Adderall, a powerful prescription medication designed to sharpen his focus and concentration. Now, let me tell you, Adderall is no ordinary medicine; it's a Schedule II controlled substance, a stimulant containing amphetamine.

Throughout high school, this boy relied on Adderall to navigate the challenges of his education. His determination, coupled with this medication, earned him a place in a prestigious college.

In his freshman year, a friend came to him with a simple request: a bit of Adderall for a late-night study session. With his compassionate heart, he agreed to help. Word spread like wildfire, and other college students sought him out for his medication. An idea began to take shape – why not turn this into an opportunity? He didn't have to pay for his medication, thanks to his condition and insurance coverage.

So, he became the go-to person for Adderall on campus. Demand skyrocketed, and the allure of quick money grew stronger.

One fateful day, a student contacted him with an unusual request: a full bottle of Adderall. The promise of substantial financial gain overwhelmed him, and he eagerly agreed to the exchange. They set a meeting downstairs from his dorm room, where he was greeted not only by a handful of cash but also a pair of handcuffs.

The excitement of profit was replaced by sheer dread as those cuffs closed around his wrists. The student was, in fact, an undercover agent, and the young boy's world came crashing down.

I share this story not as an isolated incident but as a cautionary tale that I've encountered in various forms. It serves as a reminder that actions, seemingly harmless and inconsequential, can snowball into life-altering mistakes.

This young man, once destined for a bright future, now carries a criminal record, a stark reminder that something as seemingly innocent as sharing a pill with a friend can lead to a cascade of consequences – jail time, substantial court fees and fines, and the forfeiture of a once-promising future.

Moral

We must think of our decisions like a snowball rolling down a hill. Even small choices can start a snowball effect, turning into big mistakes with serious consequences. So, always consider the potential outcomes before making decisions.

Made in the USA
Columbia, SC
10 September 2024

6a9c0b58-32ea-47bd-8ed2-dc86610967f8R01